THE WAY PEOPLE LIVE

W9-AZB-254

Life in Charles Dickens's England

by Diane Yancey

Lucent Books, P.O. Box 289011, San Diego, CA 92198-9011

Library of Congress Cataloging-in-Publication Data

Yancey, Diane.
    Life in Charles Dickens's England / by Diane Yancey.
        p.   cm. — (The way people live)
    Includes bibliographical references and index.
    Summary: Describes the people and conditions of life in England during
the time of Charles Dickens and examines how those conditions are
reflected in his work.
    ISBN 1-56006-098-0 (lib. bdg.   :   alk. paper)
    1. Dickens, Charles, 1812–1870—Contemporary England—Juvenile
literature.   2. Literature and society—England—History—19th century—
Juvenile literature.   3. Dickens, Charles, 1812–1870—Knowledge—
England—Juvenile literature.   4. England—Social life and customs—19th
century—Juvenile literature.   5. Manners and customs in literature—
Juvenile literature.   6. England—In literature—Juvenile literature.
[1. Dickens, Charles, 1812–1870.   2. England—Social life and customs—
19th century.   3. England—In literature.   4. Authors, English.]
I. Title.   II. Series.
PR4583.Y35   1999
823'.8—dc21   98-19569
                                                                        CIP
                                                                        AC

Printed in the U.S.A.

Contents

Discovering the Humanity in Us All

The Way People Live series focuses on pockets of human culture. Some of these are current cultures, like the Eskimos of the Arctic; others no longer exist, such as the Jewish ghetto in Warsaw during World War II. What many of these cultural pockets share, however, is the fact that they have been viewed before, but not completely understood.

To really understand any culture, it is necessary to strip the mind of the common notions we hold about groups of people. These stereotypes are the archenemies of learning. It does not even matter whether the stereotypes are positive or negative; they are confining and tight. Removing them is a challenge that's not easily met, as anyone who has ever tried it will admit. Ideas that do not fit into the templates we create are unwelcome visitors—ones we would prefer remain quietly in a corner or forgotten room.

The cowboy of the Old West is a good example of such confining roles. The cowboy was courageous, yet soft-spoken. His time (it is always a he, in our template) was spent alternatively saving a rancher's daughter from certain death on a runaway stagecoach, or shooting it out with rustlers. At times, of course, he was likely to get a little crazy in town after a trail drive, but for the most part, he was the epitome of inner strength. It is disconcerting to find out that the cowboy is human, even a bit childish. Can it really be true that cowboys would line up to help the cook on the trail drive grind coffee, just hoping he would give them a little stick of pep-

permint candy that came with the coffee shipment? The idea of tough cowboys vying with one another to help "Coosie" (as they called their cooks) for a bit of candy seems silly and out of place.

So is the vision of Eskimos playing video games and watching MTV, living in prefab housing in the Arctic. It just does not fit with what "Eskimo" means. We are far more comfortable with snow igloos and whale blubber, harpoons and kayaks.

Although the cultures dealt with in Lucent's The Way People Live series are often historically and socially well known, the emphasis is on the personal aspects of life. Groups of people, while unquestionably affected by their politics and their governmental structures, are more than those institutions. How do people in a particular time and place educate their children? What do they eat? And how do they build their houses? What kinds of work do they do? What kinds of games do they enjoy? The answers to these questions bring these cultures to life. People's lives are revealed in the particulars and only by knowing the particulars can we understand these cultures' will to survive and their moments of weakness and greatness.

This is not to say that understanding politics does not help to understand a culture. There is no question that the Warsaw ghetto, for example, was a culture that was brought about by the politics and social ideas of Adolf Hitler and the Third Reich. But the Jews who were crowded together in the ghetto cannot be understood by the Reich's politics. Their life was a day-to-day battle for existence, and the creativity and methods they used to prolong their lives is a vital story of human perseverance that would be denied by focusing only on the institutions of Hitler's Germany. Knowing that children as young as five or six outwitted Nazi guards on a daily basis, that Jewish policemen helped the Germans control the ghetto, that children attended secret schools in the ghetto and even earned diplomas—these are the things that reveal the fabric of life, that can inspire, intrigue, and amaze.

Books in The Way People Live series allow both the casual reader and the student to see humans as victims, heroes, and onlookers. And although humans act in ways that can fill us with feelings of sorrow and revulsion, it is important to remember that "hero," "predator," and "victim" are dangerous terms. Heaping undue pity or praise on people reduces them to objects, and strips them of their humanity.

Seeing the Jews of Warsaw only as victims is to deny their humanity. Seeing them only as they appear in surviving photos, staring at the camera with infinite sadness, is limiting, both to them and to those who want to understand them. To an object of pity, the only appropriate response becomes "Those poor creatures!" and that reduces both the quality of their struggle and the depth of their despair. No one is served by such two-dimensional views of people and their cultures.

With this in mind, The Way People Live series strives to flesh out the traditional, two-dimensional views of people in various cultures and historical circumstances. Using a wide variety of primary quotations—the words not only of the politicians and government leaders, but of the real people whose lives are being examined—each book in the series attempts to show an honest and complete picture of a culture removed from our own by time or space.

By examining cultures in this way, the reader will notice not only the glaring differences from his or her own culture, but also will be struck by the similarities. For indeed, people share common needs—warmth, good company, stability, and affirmation from others. Ultimately, seeing how people really live, or have lived, can only enrich our understanding of ourselves.

"A Terrible Boy to Read"

The England that Charles Dickens made famous in celebrated classics such as *Oliver Twist*, *David Copperfield*, and *A Christmas Carol* was a fascinating mix of mysterious fogs, grimy London streets, guileless protagonists, and unscrupulous villains. It was also a country badly in need of improvement and reform. Crime was on the rise. Pollution was widespread, and disease ran rampant. Aristocrats enjoyed lives of power and affluence in grand mansions and sprawling country estates, while the poor lived in reeking slums, worked for pennies in gloomy factories and sweatshops, and regularly died in the street from cold and hunger.

The man who entertained millions while highlighting such nineteenth-century social conditions was neither an aristocrat nor a pauper. Born on February 7, 1812, to middle-class parents who lived in Landport (now part of Portsmouth), England, Charles Dickens grew up to be a wealthy and respected man, dividing his time between a comfortable house in London, a country home near Rochester, and visits to Europe and America. Despite such a privileged lifestyle, however, the early years of his life were unsettled, and it was Dickens's good-hearted but irresponsible father who first exposed his son to many of the hardships about which he would later write.

John Dickens's continual debt eventually landed him in prison while his family struggled to make ends meet.

Debt and Disgrace

Charles Dickens's father, John Dickens, was a friendly, generous man—a clerk in the Navy Pay Office—but he was also a careless provider and continually spent more money than he earned. His creditors regularly hounded him for payment, and the family moved repeatedly to escape such annoyance. Sensitive, moody Charles wondered and worried as he grew old enough to notice the shabby homes and the pinched circumstances the family was often forced to endure.

"A Fine Little Fellow"

Although he was a member of prim and proper Victorian society, Dickens was anything but a dull, joyless character, as biographer Hesketh Pearson relates in *Dickens, His Character, Comedy, and Career*.

"The man was like his work. He was restless, vivacious, excitable, full of energy and enthusiasm, intensely aware of everything about him, highly emotional, hilarious, constantly changing in mood, now gregarious, now disposed to solitude; he laughed with those who laughed and wept with those who wept, outdoing both. . . . 'What a face is his to meet in a drawing room!' was Leigh Hunt's [editor and personal friend] first impression. . . . And [Thomas] Carlyle [writer and social philosopher], who saw him at a dinner party in the early days of his success, gives us a striking snapshot: 'He is a fine little fellow, . . . clear blue intelligent eyes that he arches amazingly, large, protrusive, rather loose mouth, a face of the most extreme *mobility*, which he shuttles about—eyebrows, eyes, mouth and all—in a very singular manner while speaking. Surmount them with a loose coil of common coloured hair, and set it on a small compact figure, very small. . . . For the rest, a quiet, shrewd-looking little fellow, who seems to guess pretty well what he is and what others are.'"

A portrait of a young Charles Dickens from an 1839 lithograph.

In late 1822, John Dickens moved his wife and children back to London, where the consequences of his overspending struck them forcibly. The family (which included six children and an orphan maid) crammed themselves into a four-room house in a poor, working-class suburb called Camden Town; Dickens would one day use it as Bob Cratchit's neighborhood in *A Christmas Carol*. Meals were skimpy since there was no money to pay the butcher and the baker. As bill collectors became more insistent, the boy was soon making innumerable trips to the neighborhood pawnshop to sell the family silver, books, and finally the furniture.

Noticing the Dickenses' penniless condition, a family friend suggested that twelve-year-old Charles earn some money by going to work at his blacking warehouse, a business in which shoe polish was manufactured and bottled. A bargain was struck, and soon, in a gloomy, rat-infested building in a section of London known as Hungerford Stairs, Dickens labored eleven hours a day over the blacking bottles. He later wrote,

> My work was to cover the pots of paste-blacking; first with a piece of oil-paper, and then with a piece of blue paper; to tie them round with a string; and then to clip the paper close and neat, all round, until it looked as smart as a pot of ointment from an apothecary's shop.[1]

Dickens became adept at his task and earned about six shillings a week, not a bad wage for a boy at the time. Charles could not make up for his father's irresponsibility, however. Less than two weeks after his son started work, John Dickens was arrested for debt and taken away to Marshalsea Prison. Following the custom of the time, his wife and children joined him there. Charles lived in rented rooms nearby so he could continue to work and run errands for his father at night. To the sensitive boy who longed to be a gentleman, this period was a constant source of humiliation, made worse by the fact that he had to give up school: "No words can express the secret agony of my soul. . . . My whole nature was . . . penetrated with . . . grief and humiliation."[2]

"Reading as If for Life"

Dickens never forgot the painful events of his early life, but this bleak period did not last long. In April 1824 John Dickens's mother died, leaving her son enough money to pay his debts and reestablish his family in Camden Town. Shortly thereafter, Charles was taken out of the blacking warehouse and enrolled at the Wellington House Academy, where he studied happily for two years, learning English, dancing, Latin, and mathematics.

There he could also indulge his love of books, which had developed when he was much younger. His nursemaid, Mary Weller, remembered him as an avid reader—"a terrible boy to read"[3] was the way she phrased it—pouring over such classics as *Don Quixote*, *Robinson Crusoe*, and the *Arabian Nights* when he was only ten years old. Dickens himself wrote of his early passion: "When I think of it, the picture always rises in my mind of a summer evening, the boys at play in the churchyard, and I sitting on my bed, reading as if for life."[4]

Hard-Hearted Woman

Despite his love of books, Dickens became convinced that money would help him become the gentleman he still longed to be, so at the age of fifteen he dropped out of school

Charles Dickens began working at Warren's Blacking Factory (building on the left) in Hungerford Stairs when he was twelve. He toiled eleven hours a day at the factory to help provide for the Dickens family.

and became a clerk in a law firm, a job he quickly found boring. Attracted by journalism, he learned shorthand with great difficulty and was hired to write for two newspapers, one of which covered the workings of Parliament. He soon earned the reputation of being the fastest and most accurate reporter in the press gallery.

In his spare time, Dickens channeled his boundless energy into a variety of pastimes and activities. He spent nights when he could not sleep exploring the slums, docks, and backwaters of London. At one of the many social events he attended, he met and fell deeply in love with beautiful, flirtatious Maria Beadnell, a banker's daughter. The romance ended unhappily for Dickens, and some suggest that the memory of Maria added to his later unhappiness with plump, blue-eyed Catherine Hogarth, whom he married in 1836. The couple had little in common, and Dickens separated from Catherine in 1858. Meeting Maria years later, he confessed, "Whatever of fancy, romance, energy, passion, aspiration and determination belong to me, I never have separated and never shall separate from the hard-hearted little woman—you—whom it is nothing to say I would have died for."[5]

An 1831 painting of Maria Beadnell, Charles Dickens's first and most passionate love. After Maria rejected him, Charles began writing magazine articles to keep his mind off the painful breakup.

Literary Success

To occupy his mind after his breakup with Maria, Dickens began writing short articles, drawing on his early childhood experiences, his London explorations, and his observation of Parliament. He had an aptitude for remembering people and places in great detail that lent realism to his work, but his ability to write depended almost entirely on his moods. His best writing was an emotional outpouring that came only after he was totally caught up in the lives of his characters. He explained, "I can never write with effect, especially in the serious way, until I have got my steam up, or in other words until I have become so excited with my subject that I cannot leave off."[6] Since his novels were published in serial form throughout his lifetime, this undisciplined style meant that he often dashed off the required twelve thousand words a month, relying on inspiration more than careful plotting or character development.

Despite their occasional flaws, Dickens's articles were quickly accepted and published by several London magazines, and they proved

Bozomania

Just as popular movies spark sales of related merchandise today, Dickens's first work generated a retail frenzy in the nineteenth century. In *Dickens, His Character, Comedy, and Career*, Hesketh Pearson details the excitement that resulted from the publication of *The Pickwick Papers* in 1836.

"Nothing like the furore caused by *Pickwick* had occurred in the history of literature. Those who did not altogether approve of it called the general excitement 'Bozomania.' There were 'Pickwick' hats, coats, canes, cigars. Dogs and cats were called 'Sam,' 'Jingle,' 'Bardell,' 'Trotter.' People were nicknamed 'Tupman,' 'Winkle,' 'Snodgrass,' 'Stiggins.' The 'Fat Boy' went into the language. The moment a monthly part was published, the cheap periodicals of the day printed long extracts from it. The work was pirated, plagiarised and dramatized, and the one person who did not benefit immediately from all this was the author, who wrote to his publishers: 'When you have quite done counting the sovereigns realised for Pickwick, I should be much obliged to you to send me up a few.'"

so popular that they were combined with a number of new pieces and published as a two-volume work in early 1836. Dickens titled them *Sketches by Boz*, Boz being the nickname of his younger brother, Augustus, and a pseudonym Dickens had previously used.

Sketches by Boz marked the beginning of Dickens's literary success. In 1836–1837, his next major work, *The Pickwick Papers*, was published in a London periodical, to be followed by episodes of *Oliver Twist* (1837–1839) and *Nicholas Nickleby* (1838–1839). From that time until his death in 1870, Dickens filled his time writing, traveling, and giving dramatic readings of his work that delighted audiences everywhere.

Dickens's England

In the course of his life, the man who began his career in a shoe-blacking warehouse went on to win great literary fame. First seen as only a storyteller, he was later recognized as a powerful writer and an astute critic of the times. He was often guilty of exaggerating the shortcomings of his fellow men, but on the whole his work dealt accurately with English life in the mid–nineteenth century. The characters he created—city men and chimney sweeps, pickpockets and politicians—together with their work, their play, their suffering, living, and dying give us a glimpse of what life was like in early Victorian England.

England and the Early Victorians

The years during which Dickens wrote, 1835–1870, turning out twenty novels and innumerable sketches and articles, were a time of great change for England. Queen Victoria ascended the throne on June 20, 1837, the year *The Pickwick Papers* was becoming a household phrase. She began her reign at the age of eighteen and ruled till the age of eighty-nine.

The queen was a wise and hardworking monarch who wanted the best for her people and knew how to delegate leadership to a series of talented prime ministers. As a result of their skilled leadership, England during the Victorian age reached the height of its economic and political power, built a great colonial empire, and instituted numerous political and social reforms at home. Dickens did not live to see all these changes, but he was there at the inception of most, and his writing helped motivate the nation to deal with many of its chronic ills.

Queen Victoria, pictured here at her first council in 1837, led England to its apex as a world power. During the years of her rule, known as the Victorian age, England was also characterized by its social problems.

Victorian England

SCOTLAND
Glasgow • Edinburgh
North Sea
North Channel
Great Britain
• Newcastle
NORTHERN IRELAND
York •
Irish Sea
Manchester •
IRELAND
Dublin •
Wolverhampton •
• Birmingham
ENGLAND
WALES   Cheltenham   Rochester
Thames R.   London •
Marlborough •
Chatham   Ramsgate
Shaftesbury •   Brighton •
Portsmouth •
Strait of Dover
English Channel
FRANCE

A Prosperous Empire

The England that Dickens knew and portrayed in his novels was a growing world power, already a landholder in North America and India. The British Empire under Victoria continued to expand until it had controlling interests in the islands of Hong Kong and Cyprus, and parts of Africa, China, and the Middle East as well. Ireland, Scotland, and Wales had already become part of Britain under the Acts of Union in 1707 and 1800.

Commerce with these regions provided brisk business for British traders and financiers, and the City of London, that part of the metropolis that lay within the boundaries of the original walled settlement, was the heart of much of this activity. A short distance away lay the London shipyards along the Thames River, miles of sprawling docks built by trading companies and other investors where ships filled with tea, silk, and tobacco from foreign ports were unloaded. Victorian journalist Henry Mayhew describes the bustling, upbeat tempo of the docks in his comprehensive study entitled *London Labour and the London Poor:*

> As you enter the dock, the sight of the forest of masts in the distance, . . . the tall chimneys vomiting clouds of black smoke, and the many coloured flags flying in the air, has a most peculiar effect. . . . The sailors are singing boisterous . . . songs from the Yankee ship just entering, . . . the ropes splash in the water; some captain shouts his orders through his hands; a goat bleats from some ship in the basin; and empty casks roll along the stones with a heavy drum-like sound.[7]

The docks were lively places, marked by shipbuilding, import/export houses, and enormous warehouses that held exotic goods such as coffee, ginger, palm oil, and rum. Foundries, sail yards, coopers yards (for barrel making), and block-and-tackle shops flourished there, while thousands of men from the poor and middle classes found work unloading freight and performing other jobs.

Industrial Revolution

England's growth and development was also stimulated by the industrial revolution, a period of social and economic development that began in the 1700s. During this period, the introduction of power-driven machines generated change in almost every facet of society.

James Watt's steam engine proved able to do the work of hundreds of horses, and with its application, steam-powered ships carried freight across the ocean faster than sailing vessels, steam locomotives linked cities and carried goods and passengers at speeds never dreamed of before, and steam-powered looms dramatically sped up textile making and made possible the mass production of garments.

Power-driven equipment sparked the development of the first factories where machines and the people who operated them came together under the same roof. Employers who recognized the benefits of such an arrangement quickly abandoned the traditional cottage industry system wherein craftspeople labored in their homes. In factories, goods were produced quickly, efficiently, and at a lower cost than ever before. Even if certain tasks were performed by hand, employees in a factory setting could be made to work longer hours at a faster pace than they would have at home.

Manufacturing and processing plants for an endless variety of products, from lampblack to glue, bonemeal to tar, soon sprang up around the country. "There are many establishments in or near London such as waterworks, gas-works, . . . tan-yards, brewhouses, distilleries, glass-works, etc., the extent of which would excite no little surprise in those who for the first time visited them,"[8] guidebook writer George Dodd wrote in 1841.

Urban Boom

With the development of industry came the growth of cities. In the 1800s, hundreds of thousands of people from farms and villages across the country moved to urban areas in the hope of finding work and improving their

---

A Rough Rhyme

While Dickens exposed the horrors of London's slums and factory towns, his contemporary Charles Kingsley focused on the plight of the rural laborer. The following ballad, taken from his 1848 novel *Yeast*, is included in Gillian Avery's *Victorian People*.

"'A Rough Rhyme on a Rough Matter'
You have sold the labouring man, squire,
   Body and soul to shame,
To pay for your seat in the House, squire,
   And to pay for the feed of your game [deer].

You made him a poacher yourself, squire,
   When you'd give neither work nor meat;
And your barley-fed hares robbed the garden
   At our starving children's feet;

When packed in one reeking chamber,
   Man, maid, mother, and little ones lay;
While the rain pattered in on the rotting bride-bed,
   And the walls let in the day;

When we lay in the burning fever
   On the mud of the cold clay floor,
Till you parted us all for three months, squire,
   At the cursed workhouse door.

We quarrelled like brutes, and who wonders?
   What self-respect could we keep,
Worse housed than your hacks [horses] and your pointers [dogs],
   Worse fed than your hogs and your sheep?"

---

lives. Surviving in the country was hard. Wealthy landowners often ignored the wages and welfare of their farm tenants, forcing most to toil endlessly and live in deepest poverty with no hope of better days ahead for themselves or their children.

London in particular experienced a population boom. In 1800, it boasted almost 1 million inhabitants; by 1881, shortly after Dickens's death, that number was 4.5 million. Some who made the move took the opportunity to become shopkeepers, servants, dressmakers, and launderers in answer to the growing demand for personal goods and services in the city. Some found work in mills, factories, and processing plants.

Thousands worked in construction, building houses, warehouses, bridges, and roads. Others helped build the railroads that tore across the once-peaceful countryside "with a shrill yell of exultation," as Dickens describes in *Dombey and Son*, "tearing on, spurning everything, . . . shrieking, roaring, rattling through the purple distance."[9] The least-fortunate newcomers joined the ranks of the vast number of poor Londoners who were not able to find work despite the wealth of opportunities the city had to offer.

Personal Effects of Revolution

Employed or unemployed, city or country dweller, the industrial revolution was a mixed blessing for early Victorians. Those with money to invest in business, manufacturing, and construction became rich from the economic boom. The average person saw job opportunities increase, was able to purchase machine-made goods and clothing at cheaper prices, and could take advantage of faster and more reliable travel. Men who could afford the daily expense of commuting by train could move their families to newly developed suburbs and thus escape the noise and dirt of inner-city life.

But the new era had serious drawbacks as well. More goods were available, but quality was often sacrificed for quantity. Life in cities was less friendly and more dangerous than in earlier times. Criminals lurked everywhere, and the growing numbers of horses, carriages, cabs, and buses created horrible traffic jams and made even crossing the street a hazardous undertaking. The cost of living in cities was high as well, and workers were at the mercy of employers who wanted to make profits at any cost. The average person labored long hours for low pay under conditions that were oppressive and unsafe.

Powerful Politicians

While the rich got richer and the poor struggled to survive, many of England's political leaders chose to ignore the negative effects of the industrial revolution. Queen Victoria had concern for her people, but she had to share authority with Parliament, and members of the powerful House of Lords—landowners and nobility—were loath to make changes that would reduce their power or diminish their wealth. Members of the less powerful House of Commons who represented the general population were often convinced (or bribed) to go along with their noble colleagues.

It was not surprising, then, that laws in Dickens's time often neglected or ignored the rights of ordinary people. Voters and candidates for Parliament were required to meet property qualifications before they could participate, a restriction that excluded women, many of the middle class, and the poor. Laws regarding representation were biased or out-

A congested street in London during the industrial revolution. As the city swelled with people, it became increasingly noisy, polluted, and dangerous.

of-date; some sparsely populated areas were well represented in Parliament, while workers in growing towns such as Manchester had no voice at all.

Coodle and Doodle

In 1832, when he was barely twenty years old, Dickens became a reporter for two newspapers, the *True Sun* and the *Mirror of Parliament*, the latter a London publication in which he reported parliamentary speeches and debates verbatim. In 1834 he took a similar position with the *Morning Chronicle*. After several months of such work, Dickens grew disillusioned with politics, drawing the conclusion that wealth rather than ability gave a man power and influence in government. He saw most members of Parliament as fools or self-serving hypocrites, more concerned with furthering their own interests and impressing their colleagues than helping the people they represented.

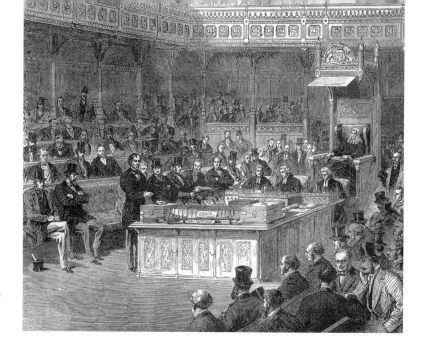

The British Parliament consisted of the House of Lords and the House of Commons (pictured). As a reporter who covered Parliament's activities, Dickens came to believe that politicians were self-serving and ineffective.

Ironically, some historic reforms were passed during the four years Dickens reported on Parliament. Slavery was abolished in British colonies. Legislation was passed that gave more citizens the vote, reduced hours in the workday, and addressed some of the needs of the poor. In practice, however, many of these laws were first steps rather than solutions, and, by the time Dickens gave up reporting in 1836, he was totally frustrated with Parliament and scorned all political posturing throughout his lifetime.

He expressed his feelings by criticizing and ridiculing government. In 1837 he wrote, "We take it that the commencement of a Session of Parliament is neither more nor less than the drawing up of the curtain for a grand comic pantomime." [10] And in *Bleak House* he poked fun at self-important members of Parliament:

> England has been in a dreadful state for some weeks. Lord Coodle would go out, Sir Thomas Doodle wouldn't come in, and there being nobody in Great Britain (to speak of) except Coodle and Doodle,

there has been no government. . . . The marvellous part of the matter is, that England has not appeared to care very much about it, but has gone on eating and drinking and marrying . . . as the old world did in the days before the flood. [11]

Dickens was repeatedly asked to run for Parliament during his lifetime. He always refused, stating that his life was dedicated to his writing, and wondering "how any man of worth can endure the personal contemplation of the House of Commons." [12]

The City

Parliament was not the only political body that angered Dickens. London was the seat of national government, but the metropolis itself had its own city government, which proved too fragmented and bound by tradition to deal effectively with the far-reaching effects of growth. The *Times* noted in 1855 that London was "rent into an affinity of divisions, districts and areas. . . . Within the metropolitan limits, the local administration is carried on by no fewer than 300 different bodies deriving powers from about 150 different local Acts."[13]

The lord mayor was head administrator of the City (old London) and its surrounding districts. Governing with him was a body known as the Corporation, made up of a court of aldermen (well-to-do bankers and heads of large businesses elected for life by London taxpayers) and a court of common council, craftsmen and tradesmen who were elected annually. This metropolitan authority tended to ignore conditions in London's fast-growing suburbs and did all it could to block reforms that it feared would lessen its power.

A second governing unit was the vestry, or parish—districts managed by councilmen who dealt with local issues such as maintenance and sanitation. Scores of vestries existed throughout London and its suburbs.

Many were well managed, others were not. An example of one of the latter was St. Pancras vestry, where 7 of the 122 vestry committeemen were noblemen and two-thirds were wealthy homeowners. With no concern for the economic burden imposed on thousands of laborers in their district, the vestrymen of St. Pancras sponsored costly projects such as the construction of an elaborate new parish church, which effectively trebled taxes. At the same time, they ignored the plight of the growing number of vagrants who were regularly hauled off to the St. Pancras Workhouse, notorious for its corrupt administration and unhealthy living conditions.

With little innovation in City government and too little coordination between vestries, creative solutions for problems such as crime, pollution, and homelessness that plagued the growing metropolis were slow in coming. And with no master plan to regulate

Political Enemies

Two political parties, the Whigs and the Tories, dominated English politics in Dickens's day. Allegiance to the former was more than a political persuasion, as Gillian Avery explains in *Victorian People*.

"The great 19th century aristocrats, one might say, belonged to the same club. And a feature of . . . this club was Whiggery—a political opinion that one did not arrive at, as a general rule, by independent thought, but which one inherited from one's family. The Whigs held certain political opinions and pursued certain policies, but people did not become Whigs because they upheld these opinions; rather they upheld them because they were born into a Whiggish family.

The two great parties of England, the Whigs and the Tories, had arisen at the end of the 17th century, and were to turn by the end of the 19th into the Liberal and the Conservative parties. Broadly speaking, the Whigs were the great landed aristocrats, the descendants of the powerful nobility . . . while the Tories . . . were the lesser landowners, together with such elements as the clergy and the manufacturers. Their hatred and suspicion of each other's political policies often went very deep. There is a story of a child of Whig parents who asked her mother whether the Tories were born bad or just grew bad. 'They are born bad and grow worse,' her mother told her with passionate feeling."

or direct growth, the expansion of London was as haphazard as it was rapid. Historian Roy Porter writes, "Population rise had never been more explosive, industry never more polluting, disruption, demolition and building more frenzied."[14]

In effect, those with money—in a letter Dickens called them "sleek, slobbering, bow-paunched, over-fed, apoplectic snorting cattle"[15]—controlled London. They built where they wanted without thought of standards or codes, barricaded public streets, and razed neighborhoods to make way for railroads and new housing developments. They tolerated corruption, put down re-forms as too risky and expensive to contemplate, and rigorously protested interference from the federal government. Only when a problem grew so threatening or public revolt seemed close at hand did Parliament step in and require reforms be made.

Radicals

With government largely unresponsive to the needs of common people, so-called radicals often spoke out in reaction to such indifference. Dickens himself was considered a radical since he constantly criticized the

Frustrated Journalist

In his youth, Dickens struggled with shorthand to become a parliamentary reporter, but he was quickly disillusioned with the political system as he grew familiar with it. The author created a protagonist whose outlook echoed his own views in his novel *David Copperfield*.

"I have tamed that savage stenographic mystery. I make a respectable income by it. I am in high repute for my accomplishment in all pertaining to the art, and am joined with eleven others in reporting the debates in Parliament for a Morning Newspaper. Night after night, I record predictions that never come to pass, professions that are never fulfilled, explanations that are only meant to mystify. I wallow in words. Britannia [Great Britain], that unfortunate female, is always before me, like a trussed fowl: skewered through and through with office-pens, and bound hand and foot with red tape. I am sufficiently behind the scenes to know the worth of political life. I am quite an Infidel about it, and shall never be converted."

A page of Dickens's shorthand notes. Both Dickens and his character David Copperfield learned shorthand with difficulty and became parliamentary reporters.

government's two main parties, the Whigs and the Tories (later the Liberals and Conservatives).

Most radicals were ordinary workingmen who seldom organized, and rarely posed a severe threat to national stability. One exception occurred in the 1840s, however, when public protest against the Corn Laws became a national outcry and brought the threat of revolution very close.

The Corn Laws, passed in 1815, were an effort to protect English farmers from unfair competition and made illegal the purchase of cheap grain from Europe. In effect, however, the new regulations kept grain prices so high in England that by the 1840s ordinary people were unable to afford food. In desperation, starving workingmen gathered at political meetings and considered drastic action. Hungry laborers set fire to farmers' hayricks. Threats were made on the life of the queen.

The national upheaval was finally taken seriously by Parliament, and the Corn Laws were repealed in 1846. William Gladstone, prime minister in 1868, remarked in retrospect, "I have no hesitation in saying that if the repeal of the Corn Laws had been defeated or even retarded, we should have had a revolution." [16]

The most organized radical group to oppose the government in the 1840s was the Chartists. Formed in the 1830s and made up of workingmen who sought to improve the hopeless conditions under which all laborers worked and lived, the group demanded voting rights for all men, secret ballot elections, fairly divided electoral districts, and the abolition of property qualifications for members of Parliament.

The Chartist cause was popular, and membership was high when economic conditions were at their worst. Support waned when conditions improved, however, and the organization died out in 1848 after a highly publicized rally in London fizzled due to apathy and a heavy rainstorm. Nevertheless, the prospect of hundreds of thousands of angry workers marching on Parliament was enough to motivate the government to bring in troops and station police around all of London's public buildings in preparation for violence that never materialized.

A Defining Part of Life

Ordinary men and women of Dickens's time did not want revolution so much as they wanted the chance to work, to earn a reasonable wage, and to gain a measure of control over their lives. As farm laborer Will Fern says in Dickens's *The Chimes*, published in 1844, "Give us . . . better homes when we're a-lying in our cradles; give us better food when we're a-working for our lives." [17]

To most early Victorians, a job was a means of survival, but it was something more as well. It was a status symbol, a safety net, a ladder to success. As in our contemporary world, jobs determined to a great extent the way people defined themselves and the kind of lives they led.

City Men and Climbing Boys

In Dickens's England, one's occupation determined where one lived, the clothes one wore, and the respect one could command in society. With enough money, a man could become a part of the upper class with all its influence and opportunity. Without skills and a decent income, he quickly slipped into a life of poverty, powerlessness, and desperation.

The Barnacles

Upper-class employment, particularly for members of the nobility, was often more of an option than a necessity. Landowners with large estates spent their days overseeing their property and the tenants who rented and farmed it, but many wealthy men simply hired a bailiff or land agent. That gave them freedom to entertain their friends and participate in sports such as hunting, riding, and horse racing. Many members of the aristocracy made membership in Parliament their career in order to oversee its workings and protect their own interests.

Among those who held positions in government, nepotism, the practice of giving jobs to relatives, was widespread. Dickens targeted nepotism in his novel *Little Dorrit* with the creation of Lord Decimus Tite Barnacle and his family, who, true to their name, were a fixture in government.

An Unfeeling Bosom

Like many of Dickens's portrayals of the rich, Mr. Merdle in *Little Dorrit* is a pompous character, concerned with appearances and loved by a society who judges him solely by his wealth and power.

"Mr. Merdle was immensely rich; a man of prodigious enterprise; a Midas without the ears, who turned all he touched to gold. He was in everything good, from banking to building. He was in Parliament, of course. He was in the City, necessarily. He was Chairman of this, Trustee of that, President of the other. The weightiest of men had said to projectors, 'Now, what name have you got? Have you got Merdle?' And the reply being in the negative, had said, 'Then I won't look at you.'

This great and fortunate man had provided that extensive bosom, which required so much room to be unfeeling enough in, with a nest of crimson and gold some fifteen years before. It was not a bosom to repose upon, but it was a capital bosom to hang jewels upon. . . . The jewels showed to the richest advantage. The bosom, moving in Society with the jewels displayed upon it, attracted general admiration. Society approving, Mr. Merdle was satisfied."

Many of the "new rich" ran their businesses focused solely on profit and disregarded their workers' well-being. Though they had climbed their way up from the working class, they opposed attempted labor reforms, claiming it would damage their businesses and the economy.

The Barnacles were a very high family, and a very large family. They were dispersed all over the public offices, and held all sorts of public places. Either the nation was under a load of obligation to the Barnacles, or the Barnacles were under a load of obligation to the nation. It was not quite unanimously settled which; the Barnacles having their opinion, the nation theirs.[18]

The Bounderbys of England

The "new rich," those men who had recently made fortunes in banking, industry, and manufacturing, were also a part of the upper class. Despite their wealth, such men were usually hardworking individuals who had achieved their position through a combination of ability, ruthlessness, and good luck, and believed that anyone who worked hard enough could enjoy similar success. They visited their businesses regularly and oversaw the work process, although most undoubtedly hired managers to cope with the daily routine.

Since the new rich were used to hard work, they also worked their employees hard and blocked attempts to improve working conditions. Businesses would fail, they argued, and the economy would collapse if the workday was shortened or money was spent to improve the workplace. The majority of Parliament agreed, and thus these captains of industry were able to amass even greater fortunes, while those they employed were reduced to a hand-to-mouth existence.

Dickens characterized the newly rich in the character of Josiah Bounderby, a heartless mill owner in *Hard Times*. Bounderby was everything that Dickens disliked: uncaring, uneducated, and self-important. "He was a rich man: banker, merchant, manufacturer, and what not. A big, loud man . . . a man made

The Law Stationer

In the broad spectrum of middle-class occupations, one of the most common was that of proprietor of a small business. In *Bleak House*, Dickens creates one such businessman, a mild-mannered individual named Snagsby who owns a law stationers shop in the heart of London.

"On the eastern borders of Chancery Lane, that is to say, more particularly in Cook's Court, Cursitor Street, Mr. Snagsby, Law-Stationer, pursues his lawful calling. In the shade of Cook's Court, at most times a shady place, Mr. Snagsby has dealt in all sorts of blank forms of legal process; in skins and rolls of parchment; in paper—foolscap, brief, draft, brown, white, whitey-brown, and blotting; in stamps, in office-quills, pens, ink, . . . and wafers; in red tape and green ferret; in short, in articles too numerous to mention. . . .

Mr. Snagsby . . . is a mild, bald, timid man with a shining head, and a scrubby clump of black hair sticking out at the back. He tends to meekness and obesity. As he stands at his door at Cook's Court, in his grey shop-coat and black calico sleeves, looking up at the clouds; or stands behind a desk in his dark shop, with a heavy flat ruler, snipping and slicing at sheepskin, in company with his two 'prentices; he is emphatically a retiring and unassuming man."

out of a coarse material . . . who was always proclaiming, through that brassy speaking-trumpet of a voice of his, his old ignorance and his old poverty."[19]

A Fast-Growing Category

Although Dickens was prejudiced against the rich and powerful, he did create sympathetic characters among the well-to-do; Mr. Brownlow in *Oliver Twist* and Mr. Jardyce in *Bleak House* were two of them. He was also indulgent in his portrayals of the middle class, particularly small businessmen, clerks, bank employees, and others who worked hard for what they earned, made the best of what they had, and did not take as great of advantage of their colleagues and dependents as did wealthier men.

Middle class was a fairly new and often confusing term in the nineteenth century. To some, it meant businessmen: individuals ranging from successful merchants and manufacturers down to simple tradesmen. For others, the term referred to the gentry, doctors, clergymen, governesses, and others who were educated and "gentlemanly born," but not aristocrats. The term eventually came to include all of the above categories, plus anyone else who did not fit into the ranks of the rich or the poor.

Dickens regularly included a sprinkling of middle-class characters in his articles and novels, making them likable people even if they have their flaws. In *Sketches by Boz*, the naive Mr. Tuggs, a grocer whose life is changed by a legacy of twenty thousand pounds, takes his family on holiday to Ramsgate, where he is duped out of part of his fortune. In *David Copperfield*, genial Mr. Micawber, an agent for a company of wine merchants, is pompous, portly, and constantly in debt, but refuses to borrow from David, whom he regards in the light of a son.

Another likable representative of the middle class was Charles Pooter, a character found in George Grossmith's popular novel

Diary of a Nobody, written in 1894. Pooter was a city man—a clerk in a London office—and his naive efforts to be "genteel" (refined) delighted thousands of readers.

Like many members of the class he represented, Pooter religiously conformed to the exacting demands of his employer, arriving at the office at an early hour and working at least ten hours a day, six days a week. He counted himself lucky to be given a lunch hour and bathroom breaks, and saw paid holidays as undreamed-of luxuries. Bob Cratchit, another city man, meekly tolerated daily insults and indignities from Scrooge in Dickens's *Christmas Carol*, and he was delighted to be allowed to celebrate Christmas Day with his family. His meekness and gratitude were fairly accurate reflections of middle-class behavior in the workplace during that time.

Making a Living

A prosperous economy supported the growth of the middle class in Dickens's England, but at the same time, unregulated wages, lack of

This illustration from David Copperfield *shows Mr. Micawber and David Copperfield. The middle class of Dickens's England was not clearly defined, but it included individuals such as Mr. Micawber, who were neither wealthy nor poor.*

job security, and exploitive employers led to increasing numbers of poor, those "down-trodden operatives, . . . the slaves of an iron-handed and a grinding despotism!"[20] as agitator Slackbridge describes them in *Hard Times*.

To the lower class, any work that paid was acceptable. The most desirable jobs, however, were those that were full-time since they provided a regular income. Occupations that fell into this category included servant, weaver, dressmaker, miner, and construction worker. Semiskilled occupations related to shipping were full-time as well, including barrel making, rope making, and carpentering.

Even if work was steady, it was by no means easy. Fourteen- to sixteen-hour days were the rule. Wages were low—twenty shillings a week or less for men, fourteen or less for women and children. Author Andrew Mearns observed in 1883:

> We ask a woman who is making tweed trousers, how much she can earn in a day, and are told one shilling. But what does a day mean to this poor soul? *Seventeen hours!* from five in the morning to ten at night—no pause for meals. She eats her crust and drinks a little tea as she works, making in very truth, with her needle and thread, not her living only, but her shroud.[21]

In many cases, working conditions were dangerous and inhumane. Injury and death were

A drawing entitled Bob Cratchit's Christmas Dinner *illustrates Dickens's* A Christmas Carol. *Like Bob Cratchit, most workers were rarely permitted to spend holidays with their families.*

Matchmakers, such as these in a factory in London's East End, were exposed to phosphorous fumes that caused an often fatal decay of the jawbones. Such dangerous working conditions were typical during Dickens's time.

common occurrences, particularly on the docks, where workers were crushed by heavy loads or drowned when they fell into the water.

Danger in the Workplace

Factories were equally hazardous. There, workers hunched over their machines for hours, performing endlessly repetitive tasks in dim, poorly heated buildings whose atmosphere was often polluted with chemicals, particles of lint, or other substances.

In the Bryant and May matchworks, girls who dipped matches were exposed daily to phosphorous fumes and developed "fossy jaw"—decay of the jawbones, which usually proved fatal. In London's boiling houses (sugar-refining plants), laborers breathed in nauseating fumes while working nearly naked in buildings that were covered with a thick black coating of sugar and grime. In an 1854 edition of his weekly magazine, *Household*

Words, founded in 1850, Dickens wrote about thousands of gory accidents that occurred in factories each year when young boys and men were crushed, mangled, or beaten to death in belts or moving pieces of machinery.

Few jobs were harder or more dangerous than those of miners in northern England who toiled long days underground to produce coal, which was burned in homes and industries throughout the country. The men, women, and children who worked in the mines daily faced the threat of cave-ins and explosions. Long-term exposure to coal dust resulted in black lung and other fatal lung diseases.

Sweatshops

With the rapid expansion of industry in the 1800s, sweatshops became popular with some employers. These shops, located in attics or upper rooms of buildings, were literally small, makeshift factories in which

A woman and a boy weigh a load of newly mined coal. Miners, as well as workers who unloaded coal at London's docks, breathed toxic coal dust and developed diseases such as black lung.

several employees worked at top speed making inexpensive clothes, boots, and other articles. In 1888, one newspaper reported a scene that was undoubtedly common earlier in the century as well:

> Besides the six workers there were in the room two women and two little girls. The latter appeared to be waiting for some fish that the mother was cooking for supper in the same room. . . . The master showed me one pair [of shoes]. I have seen some rubbish in the guise of boots and shoes, but these were the worst I have ever seen. . . . The employer's . . . constant threat seems to be that if his unfortunate slaves don't come to his terms he can get others who will.[22]

Women made up the majority of employees in sweatshops. Conditions were dirty, cramped, and unventilated, and fire was a serious threat since escape routes were usually a narrow flight of stairs. Many shops became death traps when a spark from a candle or

stove ignited clutter on the floor and sent a wooden building up in flames.

Sweatshops, especially those run by poor immigrants who were skilled craftsmen but had no capital to set up a larger business, drew public outcry from reformers and competitors who often used any excuse to try to stem the flow of immigrants into the country. Parliament, however, did not respond, pointing out that the country's economy might be affected if sweatshop production was cut off.

Coal Whippers

For that segment of the poor who could not find full-time employment, seasonal and part-time opportunities were available. In London, dock labor of all kinds was an option, and untold numbers of men worked transporting cargo to warehouses, carrying messages, doing maintenance and repair work, and performing other odd jobs. Stevedores unloaded ships of seasonal imports: China tea in July and November, wool in February and July, sugar and grain in September and April. Brawny "coal whippers" unloaded coal from ships and barges that arrived from Newcastle and the Midlands. The work was filthy and grueling, as one man testified:

> The dust gets into the throat, and very nearly suffocates you. You can scrape the coal-dust off the tongue with the teeth, and do what you will it is impossible to get the least spittle into the mouth. I have known the coal-dust to be that thick in a ship's hold, that I have been unable to see my mate, though he was only two feet from me.[23]

Coal workers had reputations as heavy drinkers, both to wash away the dust and to reward themselves at the end of a backbreaking day.

At times of the year when work was scarce, competition for available jobs on the docks became fierce and desperate. Crowds of men fought, bit, tore, and trampled one another in their efforts to be chosen by labor contractors; the disappointed were turned away daily in droves. Henry Mayhew writes, "[It was] a sight to sadden the most callous, to see thousands of men struggling for only one day's hire."[24]

Costermongers, Odd Men, and Boardmen

Those men who were not strong enough or lucky enough to find work on the docks sometimes found opportunities driving cabs and water carts, delivering coal, serving as night watchmen, or pasting advertisements on walls. Street vending—selling goods of all kind from an open cart on the street—was a common form of employment. Wares ranged from cheap perfume and imitation jewelry to delicacies such as roasted chestnuts and hot eels. A Londoner remembered one booth located on Whitechapel Road:

> Here are displayed all kinds of things; bits of second hand furniture, such as the head of a wooden bed . . . skates sold cheap in summer, light clothing in winter; workmen's tools of every kind, . . . books, boots, shoes, . . . cutlery, hats and caps; rat-traps and mouse-traps and birdcages; flowers and seeds, . . . bloaters and haddocks.[25]

Costermongers (fruit sellers), flower sellers, and others hawked their seasonal wares in street markets and on isolated street corners, announcing their arrival by their repeated calls of "Rushes green," and "Strawberries ripe and cherries in the rise."[26] In London, many set up their stands in Covent Gardens, the city's largest and most well known flower mart. Vendors were sometimes joined by shoeblacks, chair menders, street musicians, and antique dealers, all of whom depended on the whim of passersby to lay out a few coins for the goods and services provided.

"Odd men" worked in conjunction with market vendors, earning their name because they were hired on commission to perform odd jobs such as setting up stands, unloading produce, and delivering parcels. Though their hours and wages were uncertain, odd men often had the advantage of being paid twice, once by the vendor who hired them and once by the purchaser when they made their delivery.

"Boardmen" were hired by businesses, theaters, and carnivals to walk the streets sandwiched between two boards that advertised an upcoming event. The job was relatively undemanding, as Adolphe Smith comments in his article "The London Boardmen":

Few men who earn their living in the streets are better [more] abused and more persistently jeered at than the unfortunate individuals who let themselves out for hire as walking advertisements. The work is so hopelessly simple, that any one who can put one foot before the other can undertake it, and the carrying of boards has therefore become a means of subsistence open to the most stupid and forlorn of individuals.[27]

Dustmen

The duties of dustmen were more unpleasant than that of odd men or boardmen, but the occupation ranked relatively high in importance for one reason. Dustmen were the garbage collectors of Dickens's age, and thus were vital to everyone's health and comfort as they drove their carts through the city picking up piles of dirt, ashes, refuse, and dung that were left outside homes and on streets each day. Carting the "dust," as it was called, was a noisome task, and the comings and goings of the dust cart could be traced by the smell—the "moldy taint"—that surrounded it. The job paid relatively well, however, for those who took their work seriously and realized their importance to the community. One enterprising man charged five hundred pounds a year for carting away a parish's refuse.

Dust itself was a valuable commodity. Once sorted, its components could be sold, with ashes going to brick makers, soot and dung to companies that made commercial fertilizer, and old iron utensils and biscuit tins marketed to tin box and trunk makers for use as reinforcing corners. Even dead cats could be sold for their

Vendors sold all kinds of merchandise from their street carts or market stands, including food, furniture, tools, books, and clothes. Here, a fish peddler advertises his wares to prospective customers.

skins, which could be made into clothing. Independent scavengers—often women—made a living retrieving articles of value such as teaspoons, jewelry, iron, rags, and bones from public dustheaps. As author Millicent Rose writes, "With their skirts tucked up under stout leather aprons, they stood knee-deep in the filthy stuff they examined. Tedious as the work was, every sorter knew of someone who had found a gold chain or a diamond brooch, and could hope to be as lucky herself."[28]

In *Our Mutual Friend*, Dickens uses dust symbolically to make the point that wealth in the Victorian age often came contaminated by corruption and exploitation. His character Noddy Boffin, the Golden Dustman, buys his way into society with his enormous fortune that is literally the mountainous piles of refuse—"coal-dust, vegetable-dust, bone-dust, crockery dust, rough dust, and sifted dust"[29]—that surround his home.

Toshers

Toshing, or sewer hunting, was another job option for those individuals who did not mind foul environments. Those who pursued it entered London's large sewer pipes, then dug through the muck around their feet for coins and other articles of value that dropped out of people's pockets and made their way down the drains. Such treasures could sometimes bring in two pounds a week, a fabulous sum in the eyes of the poor. One tosher explained: "I'd put down my arm to my shoulder in the mud and bring up shillings and half-crowns, and lots of coppers, and plenty of other things. I once found a silver jug as big as a quart pot, and often found spoons and knives and forks and every thing you could think of."[30]

Toshers lived a perilous life, braving cave-ins, flash floods, poisonous air, and ferocious

"Dust" was a source of income for those who sorted it and sold the components to manufacturers. Many Londoners also combed though dustheaps in search of valuable articles such as jewelry.

rats in their search for treasure, but as a rule they were a healthy group. Many even enjoyed the life, as one man informed Henry Mayhew: "The reason I likes this sort of life is, 'cause I can sit down when I likes, and nobody can't order me about."[31]

Women's Work

Wages for the poor were so low that a family often could not survive on a single income alone. Thus, many women also went out to work every day, filling a variety of positions that were as demanding as those held by husbands, fathers, and brothers.

Victorian women often held jobs to help their families survive, earning money as laundresses (pictured), seamstresses, cooks, and maids.

Thousands of women worked as seamstresses, laundresses, or craftspeople in their homes, cooking and raising children amid a litter of garments, pins and needles, and other tools of their trade. Other women worked in small family businesses, sweatshops, or factories making buttons, brushes, perfume, even surgical instruments. Those with good manners could find positions as nursemaids and abigails (lady's maids) for the well-to-do. Enormous numbers preferred to put their homemaking skills to work and hired themselves out as cooks and charwomen (housecleaners).

Many women who were driven by extreme poverty or the desire for quick riches turned to prostitution, which often netted them more than they could earn doing honest labor. Others put their children to work, since child labor was an accepted practice in Dickens's time, and poor families needed all the help they could get to make ends meet.

Child Labor

The sight of children as young as six or seven toiling side by side with adults in the workplace was not uncommon in the Victorian era. Dickens, who remained emotionally scarred by his experience in the blacking warehouse, deplored child labor and exposed its evils in several novels. For instance, Dickens's young hero Oliver Twist is apprenticed to an undertaker in whose gruesome establishment he not only works but sleeps: "The shop was close and hot; and the atmosphere seemed tainted with the smell of coffins. The recess beneath the counter in which his flock mattress was thrust, looked like a grave."[32]

Victorian employers, not as sensitive as Dickens to the physical and emotional damage child labor could inflict, saw only the benefits to be had in hiring children. First, they were nimble, and their small hands and slender bodies could easily slip into cramped spaces. Second, children were powerless and were not likely to organize and agitate for better working conditions.

Sweeps, Miners, and Mudlarks

Chimney sweeping was one of the most notorious and brutal forms of child labor in early Victorian England. Millions of chimneys existed in London alone, many of them several stories tall and each having to be cleaned regularly. Young boys apprenticed to master sweeps were trained to climb inside and scrape away the soot and creosote. Burns, falls, and suffocation were constant dangers. Reformers and other caring individuals regularly protested the abuse, but others defended the practice, arguing that the curves and crevasses of tall chimneys could not be well cleaned by machinery, and the narrowness of the flues prevented most men from doing the job.

Children who worked in the mines suffered equally brutal conditions. In 1842 an investigation commissioned by Victorian reformer Lord Shaftesbury found that children as young as five were sent down into the low, airless passages of coal mines to load and haul cars. Girls as well as boys were employed; their work hours ranged from twelve to sixteen hours a day. The report described the children as "Chained, belted, harnessed like dogs, . . . black, saturated with wet, and more than half-naked, crawling upon their

Chimney Sweeps

Orphans such as Oliver in Dickens's *Oliver Twist* were often placed in a workhouse until they were old enough to earn their living. Though life in these charitable asylums was cruel, life as an apprentice that sometimes followed could be worse, as Ivor Brown illustrates in *Dickens in His Time*.

"The workhouse children were . . . disposed of by apprenticeship, which was a kind word for selling into slavery. . . . A deal with a master-sweep was a common way to this piece of salesmanship. The usual age for the start on a new life was six or seven; sometimes it was even earlier. The mites were first taught to follow a senior boy up the chimneys; the smaller the novice the better, since the chimneys were often extremely narrow. What was tactfully called 'repugnance' to this training, in other words natural panic at the prospect of the dirt, the darkness, and the danger of a fall or suffocation, was cured by digging pins under the learners' feet or even by lighting a fire under them. They suffered from severe sores . . . caused by continual rubbing against the chimney-walls and they became deformed by the ceaseless twisting and squirming on their way up. They were inevitably covered in soot and only at rare intervals were they bathed and scrubbed."

Children haul coal in the cramped passage of an English coal mine. An 1842 report on the horrific conditions under which young children worked prompted Parliament to restrict child labor in mines to boys older than ten.

hands and knees, and dragging their heavy loads behind them."[33] As a result of the report, Parliament outlawed female labor in the mines and prohibited boys younger than ten from being employed for that purpose.

Not every child was forced to endure such appalling conditions, but most worked hard for the money they earned. Sons and daughters as young as four regularly helped in small family businesses—delivering messages and parcels, sewing, and making toys, birdcages, and other trinkets. Many young boys like Jo in Dickens's *Bleak House* worked as crossing sweeps, earning tips for brushing aside the dust and dung that plagued pedestrians trying to cross city streets.

Some parents regularly sent their children to a neighborhood "job market" where they were hired for the day by cabinetmakers, weavers, shoemakers, and other craftsmen. The children of the destitute who lived along the river spent their days "mudlarking," combing the muddy banks for bits of coal, rope, and old iron, which could be sold for food and fuel.

Different Worlds

The early Victorian era was an age of city men and climbing boys. It was also the age of grand manors and foul inner-city slums. When England moved into the industrial age, the gap between wealth and poverty became wider than ever before. Dickens emphasized that gap when he contrasted the life of aristocratic Lady Dedlock in *Bleak House* with that of Jo the crossing sweep who lives in "a black, dilapidated street, avoided by all decent people."[34] For all intents and purposes, the rich and the poor lived in two different worlds in nineteenth-century England.

3 Londoners at Their Firesides

Nowhere could the contrast between the lifestyles of the rich and poor be better observed than in London, home of Parliament, playground of the wealthy, and the hope of immigrants and rural laborers. The capital boasted select neighborhoods distinguished by tall, gracious homes, as well as theaters, clubs, plush hotels, and modern shops that were regularly patronized by the rich. But London was also notorious for its slums, its abject poverty, and its crime. Dickens's friend Thomas Carlyle critiqued the city when he wrote in 1824:

I had much rather visit London . . . than live in it. There is in fact no life in it that I can find: the people are situated here like plants in a hothouse. . . . It is the case with all ranks: the carman with his huge slouch-hat hanging half-way down his back, consumes his breakfast of bread and tallow or hog's lard . . . along the streets. . . . The fashionable lady rises at three in the afternoon, and begins to live towards midnight. Between these two extremes, the same false and tumultuous manner of existence more or less infests all ranks.[35]

Charles Dickens's house at Gad's Hill near Rochester, about twenty-five miles southeast of London. Dickens used the country home to retreat from the bustle of city life and focus on his writing.

"Crimson and Gold"

Every facet of life was affected by one's social status in Dickens's England. The fashionable upper class lived indulgent and leisurely lives in spacious, elaborately furnished mansions such as the one owned by Sir Leicester Dedlock in Dickens's *Bleak House*. "A goodly show he makes, lying in a flush of crimson and gold, in the midst of the great drawing-room, before his favourite picture of my Lady.... Outside, the stately oaks, rooted for ages in the green ground ... bear witness to his greatness." [36]

Such dwellings were usually built in select neighborhoods in the West End of London, that region lying roughly west of the City. Dickens, when he became wealthy, purchased Tavistock House in Tavistock Square, a secluded London neighborhood. Like other well-to-do people, he also owned a gracious country home, Gad's Hill Place, which he visited whenever he wanted to concentrate on his writing.

Homes of the wealthy could be up to five stories tall, were usually built in classical style, and were outfitted with all manner of modern conveniences, including "hot and cold water, ... encaustic tiles [patterned in contrasting colors], stained glass and marble fenders." [37] Upkeep of such large homes usually required the services of a cook, butler, and housekeeper plus chambermaids, footmen, valets, and gardeners. Most women hired a nanny and a governess to care for younger children. (Dickens employed a governess for his two daughters.) Grooms and stablehands cared for the many horses that were indispensable for riding, hunting, and drawing carriages.

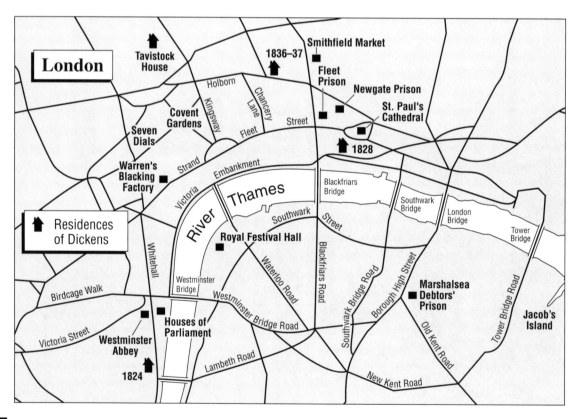

Florence Nightingale inspects a soldiers' hospital during the Crimean War. Nightingale overhauled the medical profession in England, improving hospital conditions and earning respect for women nurses.

Etiquette and Marriage

Social correctness was an imperative of the upper class, and from an early age children learned how to speak, think, and act with poise and refinement. Etiquette was more than good table manners. It was the knowledge that a well-bred gentleman never boasted of his wealth, that a lady was always polite but never familiar with her servants, and a thousand other similar conventions. So subtle yet pervasive were these practices that the newly rich never fully comprehended some of them and thus were only tolerated in upper-class circles.

For wealthy women, social correctness generally meant coping with hours of boredom. Only men worked outside the home, so wives and daughters passed the time shopping, visiting friends, doing needlework, practicing their music, or playing with their children. Florence Nightingale, a member of the upper class, proved a notable exception to this group when she embraced nursing as a ca-

reer, thus exposing herself to squalid conditions that no well-bred woman would presumably tolerate. She persisted despite the passionate protests of her family and instituted reforms that changed nursing from a haphazard practice carried out by untrained amateurs into an honorable and worthwhile profession.

For thousands of upper-class women, finding eligible husbands for marriageable daughters was an all-consuming occupation, since marriage was every woman's goal. A family with a daughter who was "coming out"—making her social debut—made it a point to be in London for the social season of May, June, and July, when all who were prominent in society attended the many social functions the capital had to offer. Ambitious mothers took advantage of those months to show off their daughters and to introduce them to the most fashionable young men of the town.

Mothers usually played a significant role in promoting romances with eligible bachelors—those with good looks, good families, and plenty of money—and steering their daughters away from ineligible ones. Younger sons fell into the latter category. In Dickens's time, the eldest son fell heir to his father's money and estates, while younger sons were given an allowance and encouraged to earn a living in the military or the church. Such young men not only lacked the resources needed to support an upper-class wife, they were often deeply in debt as a result of trying to maintain their upper-class tastes—horse racing, card playing, attending the theater, and visiting Europe—on an inadequate income.

Climbing the Social Ladder

Even after he became wealthy, Dickens identified himself with the middle class, and he remained convinced that their ambition—like his own—centered on climbing the rungs of the social ladder. In his early *Sketches by Boz*, he writes, "The wish of persons in the humbler classes of life, to ape the manners and customs of those whom fortune has placed above them, is often the subject of remark."[38]

Some believed Dickens's assessment of the middle class was too harsh, but, in fact, their lives *were* generally scaled-down versions of those of the wealthy. Middle-class homes were just as profusely decorated, but with less expensive carpets, drapes, and knickknacks. Middle-class clothes echoed styles popular with the rich. Middle-class meals, like those of the rich, emphasized meat and alcoholic beverages, and hostesses took great pride in serving an abundance of food, perhaps believing that quantity could make up for whatever their meals lacked in quality. Dickens details one such heavy repast in his novel *Martin Chuzzlewit.*

The table [groaned] beneath the weight . . . of boiled beef, roast veal, bacon, pies,

and [an] abundance of such heavy vegetables as are favourably known to housekeepers for their satisfying qualities. Besides which, there were bottles of stout, bottles of wine, bottles of ale, and divers other strong drinks, native and foreign.[39]

Despite such profusion, middle-class housewives made do with poor grades of beef, hid cheap fish under heavy sauces, and offered their guests beer instead of fine wine. Mediocre cooks, hired because they demanded lower wages than French chefs, often embarrassed their employers by producing unappetizing dishes such as Dickens describes in his sketch "The Boarding House." "Mrs. Tibbs directed James to take off the covers. Salmon, lobster sauce, giblet soup, and the usual accompaniments were *dis*-covered: potatoes like petrifactions, and bits of toasted bread, the shape and size of blank dice."[40]

Since few of the middle class ever glimpsed the private lives of the wealthy, they could only guess at the manners and routines they were trying to copy. Their pretensions were humorous to Dickens, who re-created them in *Sketches by Boz.* In "A Passage in the Life of Mr. Watkins Tottle," Mr. Tottle solemnly pretends to visit his wine cellar although he rents upstairs rooms in a lodging house. In "Sentiment," the Miss Crumptons who run a "finishing establishment for young ladies" out of their home "were very precise, had the strictest possible ideas of propriety, wore false hair, and always smelt very strongly of lavender."[41]

Villas and Boardinghouses

As London expanded and inner-city neighborhoods fell into decay, many middle-class families moved to London's fast-growing suburbs. During Dickens's time they moved there in droves, particularly after railroads and omnibuses made commuting easier.

Middle-class homes varied widely in price, size, and style. Some of the newest and best were called "villas" to convey the impression of upper-class status, although they were only moderately sized with a small garden behind. Around the middle of the century, these villas could sometimes be purchased for as little as thirty pounds. Not every family could afford a new home, but a successful craftsman could rent an older house for less than eight shillings a week, slightly less than half his weekly pay. Lower-paid workers and their families paid two to three shillings a week for a room in older houses that had been subdivided into apartments.

Boardinghouses were popular middle-class residences patronized by widows and their daughters, unmarried clerks, and other individuals who could not afford a private home. Some boardinghouses catered to the genteel middle class. In *Sketches by Boz*, Dickens's Mrs. Timms only rents to refined clientele such as the charming Mrs. Maplesone and her daughters. Other boardinghouses were dingy establishments set in a maze of London's alleyways, such as the one run by Mrs. Todgers in Dickens's *Martin Chuzzlewit*.

M. Todgers's Commercial Boarding-House was a house of that sort which is likely to be dark at any time; but that morning it was especially dark. There was

The common lodging house (pictured) was generally cheap, shabby, and occupied by the lowest members of the social ladder.

an odd smell in the passage, as if the concentrated essence of all the dinners that had been cooked in the kitchen since the house was built, lingered at the top of the kitchen stairs to that hour.[42]

Dismal and decaying "common" lodging houses, even more squalid than Todgers's, were rented by the very poor and served as dwellings for prostitutes, gamblers, and other criminals.

Respectability

Just as social correctness was important to the well-to-do, gentility and respectability were the creed of the middle class. Not only did they try to copy the upper class in matters of dress, behavior, and taste, but many believed that a

solemn and moralistic outlook was pleasing to God, the queen, and any aristocrat they might happen to meet. As Gillian Avery explains, "Respectability became a fetish, and so entangled with religious observance that few could say where genuine piety ended and a wish to stand well in the eyes of one's fellows began."[43]

To conform to such standards, many gave up relatively innocent pastimes such as dancing, cardplaying, and the theater. They became pious, intolerant, and overprotective of wives and daughters, as well as strict observers of the Sabbath. In *Little Dorrit*, Dickens paints an ugly picture of this type of family and the effect such piety had on their children:

> There was the sleepy Sunday of his boyhood, when . . . he was marched to chapel
> . . . three times a day. . . . There was the

Much of the middle class adhered devoutly to religion as a social convention, fastidiously saying prayers, reading the Bible, attending church, and avoiding any activities that might compromise their moral standing.

Middle-class families usually spent their evenings together at home partaking in conversation, reading, games, and music.

interminable Sunday of his [youth]; when his mother, stern of face and unrelenting of heart, would sit all day behind a bible. . . . There was the resentful Sunday of a little later, when he sat glowering and glooming through the tardy length of the day . . . [with] no more real knowledge of the . . . New Testament, than if he had been bred among idolaters.[44]

Cribbage and Conversation

Despite this straitlaced attitude, many members of the middle class enjoyed a variety of innocent pastimes. Families spent evenings at home talking, reading, or playing games such as cribbage and whist, a forerunner of bridge. Dickens describes such an evening in *Boz's* "The Boarding House."

Mr. Hicks and the ladies discoursed most eloquently about poetry, and the theatres. . . . The Miss Maplesones sang the most fascinating duets, and accompanied themselves on guitars, ornamented with bits of ethereal blue ribbon. . . . Mr. Tibbs spent the evening in his usual way—he went to sleep, and woke up, and went to sleep again.[45]

Many families enjoyed riding and boating, and couples occasionally took in a concert or treated themselves to an evening at the theater. Seaside holidays (vacations) were also popular with those who had time and money to get away. Preferred retreats included Brighton, known for its appeal to those with "class," and the town of Ramsgate, frequented by genteel families of moderate means such as the Tuggs in Dickens's *Sketches by Boz.*

Rough Travel

All holiday-goers had to travel to their destination, but while the rich journeyed in first-

On June 9, 1865, Dickens was involved in a railway accident while returning to London from a trip to Paris. The incident left him profoundly shaken, but he was able to write the details to a friend, Thomas Mitton, four days later. The letter, a portion of which follows, is included in *Selected Letters of Charles Dickens*, edited by David Paroissien.

"I was in the only carriage that did not go over into the stream. It was caught upon the turn by some of the ruin of the bridge, and hung suspended and balanced in an apparently impossible manner. . . . Fortunately I got out with great caution and stood upon the step. Looking down I saw the bridge gone, and nothing below me but the line of rail. Some people in the two other compartments were madly trying to plunge out of [the] window, and had no idea that there was an open swampy field fifteen feet down below them, and nothing else. . . .

[Sometime later] I came upon a staggering man covered with blood. . . . I poured some water over his face and gave him some drink, then gave him some brandy, and laid him down on the grass, and he said, 'I am gone,' and died afterwards. Then I stumbled over a lady lying on her back against a little pollard-tree. . . . The next time I passed her she was dead. . . . No imagination can conceive the ruin of the carriages, or the extraordinary weights under which the people were lying, or the complications into which they were twisted up among iron and wood, mud and water."

class luxury on the train or in private carriages, merchants, clergymen, clerks, and their families jolted endlessly in the stagecoach or packed themselves into crowded second-class railway accommodations.

Dickens regularly traveled by rail, but he disliked railroads, not only because they were dirty and noisy but because he was involved in a serious railway accident in 1865. In it, ten people were killed and twenty wounded. The author acted with great presence of mind during the accident, but for months afterward he was nervous about railway travel, and perhaps never totally recovered from the incident.

Dickens and other middle-class Victorians were used to rough travel, however, since most roads were rutted and unpaved, and vehicles were relatively crude and horse-drawn. Public transportation in London included notoriously overcrowded omnibuses, drawn by three horses and designed to carry twelve to twenty passengers. Hansom cabs, which appeared in 1834, were two-wheeled, one-horse vehicles that carried two passengers with the driver overhead, while the four-wheeled cabs, large enough to carry luggage, were nicknamed "growlers" because drivers were notoriously outspoken and rude.

Prejudice and Hardship

Like the middle class who struggled for position and respect in a society that worshiped wealth, the poor were anxious to differentiate themselves from their less respectable, more destitute neighbors. Clothing was sometimes used to indicate economic status, as Gillian Avery points out.

What a gap there was . . . between the mechanic with his collar attached to a flannel shirt and just visible along the top of a black tie, and the shopman who proudly modelled his collars on the styles affected by the aristocracy. . . . The navvy, the scaffolder, the costermonger, the cab-tout—all of them would indicate by the way they folded or knotted their neck attire the social difference of which they themselves were acutely aware.[46]

Background and race were also defining factors. The native cockney Englishman—streetwise, adaptable, and determined—saw himself as superior to the bewildered rural laborer who came to the city in the hope of a better life. Both looked down on the hundreds of thousands of "foreigners" who made up a fast-growing portion of London's population by midcentury. Many of these were Irish;

others were European Jews, and Chinese who had been sailors or ships' launderers. All faced prejudice and hardship as they tried to make their way in a society that had little concern for its own populace, let alone those of other countries.

Spartan Lifestyles

For many of the poor who settled in the East End of London—that region lying roughly east of the City—finding a home was difficult. Rents were high, wages were low, and, with the coming of railroads, entire lower-class neighborhoods were demolished to make way for miles of track. In 1836 alone, almost three thousand dwellings were razed during the building of the London and Blackwall railway.

An illustration from 1879 shows a landlord visiting a tenant family in their modest apartment. Life for many of London's poor was an unrelenting struggle to earn enough money to pay the often high rent and buy basic necessities.

The *Times* of London deplored such destruction in an article in 1861: "The poor are displaced, but they are not removed. They are shovelled out of one side of the parish, only to render more overcrowded the stifling apartments in another part."[47]

Those who could find housing made do with fewer than four rooms, which were usually cold in winter and hot in summer. Furnishings were sparse, although some families brightened their surroundings with fresh flowers, inexpensive watercolor pictures, and cheap china ornaments. In Dickens's *Tale of Two Cities*, Jerry Cruncher and his family live in two rooms, "but they were very decently kept. . . . The room in which he lay abed was already scrubbed throughout; and between the cups and saucers arranged for breakfast [on] the lumbering deal table, a very clean white cloth was spread."[48]

Paying for even such spartan accommodations took up a large proportion of a man's wages, and families such as the Crunchers were chronically short of money. Food had to be the cheapest available, usually sausage, cabbage, bread, tea, and beer. Clothes came from pawnbroker shops and secondhand stores, which flourished due to the high demand for castoffs.

Any emergency could plunge a family into debt and destitution, but most managed to cope, and even splurge on an occasional small pleasure such as a birthday present or a treat of seedcake and jam when a guest came to dinner. While most parents still had the time and energy to show affection to each other and to their offspring, the most destitute found life a hopeless business and children a burden rather than a blessing.

"Shabby-Genteel"

One segment of the respectable poor who teetered on the brink of hopelessness was, in Dickens's words, "shabby-genteel" people, tragic individuals who had once been members of the educated middle class but who, for various reasons such as alcoholism or illness, were out of work. Shabby-genteel people lived in the cheapest of rooms and survived on meager earnings from part-time work such as tutoring, debt collecting, copying legal documents, and the like.

In *Sketches by Boz*, Dickens identified shabby-genteel people by their unsuccessful attempts to hide their poverty. Their clothes were clean and neat, but threadbare. Old suits or hats were often "revived" with cheap dye in an attempt to make them appear new again. In order to appear busy and purposeful, shabby-genteels always carried books or an umbrella, as if they were coming to or going from work. To Dickens, however, their embarrassed demeanor betrayed them: "A glance at that depressed face, and timorous air of conscious poverty, will make your heart ache. . . . [The shabby-genteel person] is one of the most pitiable objects in human nature."[49]

The Rookeries

The poorest of the poor, those who could not afford even the meager comfort of a small home, usually found shelter in one of London's notorious "rookeries," slums that boasted such colorful names as Rosemary Lane and Jacob's Island.

These grim, deteriorating environs, some of which lay just across a thoroughfare from well-to-do neighborhoods, were anything but colorful. Within their boundaries, thousands of people crowded together in the most appalling living conditions imaginable. In *Sketches by Boz*, Dickens describes the streets and alleys of one of the most infamous, Seven Dials, writing of its filthy alleys, its dingy rag

Dickens was at his best when describing the slums of London, and he colorfully does so in *Oliver Twist*, as the Artful Dodger leads Oliver through back streets and alleys to be introduced to that "pleasant old gentleman," Fagin.

"Although Oliver had enough to occupy his attention in keeping sight of his leader, he could not help bestowing a few hasty glances on either side of the way, as he passed along. A dirtier or more wretched place he had never seen. The street was very narrow and muddy; and the air was impregnated with filthy odours. There were a good many small shops, but the only stock in trade appeared to be heaps of children, who, even at that time of night, were crawling in and out at the doors, or screaming from the inside. The sole places that seemed to prosper, amid the general blight of the place, were the public-houses; and in them, the lowest orders of Irish were wrangling with might and main. Covered ways and yards, which here and there diverged from the main street, disclosed little knots of houses, where drunken men and women were positively wallowing in the filth; and from several of the doorways, great ill-looking fellows were cautiously emerging; bound, to all appearance, on no very well-disposed or harmless errands."

and bone shops, and its destitute inhabitants. "The streets and courts dart in all directions, until they are lost in the unwholesome vapour which hangs over the house tops." [50]

Dickens drew on his knowledge of Seven Dials and other slum neighborhoods when he created Tom-all-Alone's, a fictional London rookery in *Bleak House*, where buildings collapse without warning and children wander the streets looking for shelter.

These tumbling tenements contain, by night, a swarm of misery. As on the ruined human wretch, vermin parasites appear, so, these ruined shelters have bred a crowd of foul existence that crawls in and out of gaps in walls and boards; and coils itself to sleep, in maggot numbers, where the rain drips in. [51]

Some people in such neighborhoods undoubtedly tried to keep their miserable rooms as clean as possible, but most did nothing to combat the decay and squalor. Overcrowding was severe; to make a few pennies, families often sublet their lodgings to other families, resulting in dozens of people living in two or three tiny rooms. Sanitation facilities were nonexistent. Back alleys served as toilets, and garbage was thrown into the street. The resulting stench was overpowering, particularly in hot weather, and visitors not used to the smells often gagged and vomited when they entered the environs.

"The Misery I See"

In the rookeries, life was a helter-skelter affair, affected in every way by the mean and colorless surroundings. There were no yards or parks, so children grew up playing in the filthy alleyways and gutters. Women gossiped and argued with each other from their doorways, which were always open to let in what little light filtered between the close-packed

Bedraggled residents of a ramshackle building spill out onto the street in a rookery in the Whitechapel neighborhood of London. Streets and alleys in such slums were filled with human waste and other garbage.

buildings. Men with nothing to do lounged on street corners or passed the time at the neighborhood tavern.

At night, screams and shouts filled the air. Abuse, crime, and alcoholism touched many families, and while early marriages were common, good relationships were not. Dickens points out, "Alas! the man in the shop ill treats his family; the carpet beater extends his professional pursuits to his wife, . . . the Irishman comes home drunk every other night, and attacks everybody; and the one-pair back screams at everything."[52]

Starvation was as great a threat as the epidemics of disease that swept the rookeries periodically. An East End doctor, one of few medical authorities to serve the poor, remarked,

The whole of the East End is starving. . . . I do not mean to say they have no bread. But they are all underfed. . . . I bring into the world scrofulous children [children who have tuberculosis of the lymph nodes]; I bolster up diseased patients; I let people down easily in the grave; I do no good, but I cannot go away. The misery I see binds me here as a parish doctor.[53]

Cadgers

Doomed to penury, the poor did anything they could to survive. Many lived by petty thievery, snatching a piece of fruit or a pie from a cart when the vendor was not looking. Others became "cadgers," street beggars who slept in doorways and alleys and usually kept a pathetic-looking child by their side to garner coins from sympathetic passersby. A great number of beggars were homeless children who had been abandoned by their parents. French critic and historian Hippolyte Taine described those he saw on a walk along the Thames River.

The whole place is alive with 'street-boys', bare-footed, filthy, turning cartwheels for a penny. They swarm on the stairs down to the Thames, more stunted, more livid, more deformed, more repulsive than the street urchins of Paris; the climate, of course, is worse, and the gin murderous.[54]

As an alternative to begging, young women in desperate straits turned to prostitution, while homeless mothers hoping to provide a better life for their children sometimes sold their babies to anyone who would pay. Ironically, unscrupulous buyers often took out a life insurance policy on their new acquisition, then allowed it to starve to death in order to collect the insurance. After its inception in 1878, the Salvation Army sent workers onto the streets to intercept baby-sellers, who were happy to place their children in responsible hands. "They know that we have a home for children at Clapton," reported one worker. "They say, 'You can bring them up to earn a decent living. We have nothing for them to eat, and with us they must see a deal of wickedness. Take them to your Home, and give them a proper start.'"[55]

Fate Worse than Death

When life became unbearable and the poor had no other option, they reluctantly entered the workhouse, an institution originally created

---

Cadgers' Talk

Many of the poor spoke a language of their own, comprised of curious jingles, words spelled backwards, and rhyming slang. In his multivolume work, *London Labour and the London Poor*, Victorian author and observer Henry Mayhew records a conversation with a London beggar who helped explain a few of the mysteries of that language.

"The cadgers' talk is quite different now to what it was in the days of Billy [in the reign of William IV]. You see the flats got awake to it, so in course we had to alter the patter.

The new style of cadgers' cant is nothing like the thieves' cant and is done all on the rhyming principle. This way's the caper. Suppose I want to ask a pal to come and have a *glass of rum* and smoke a *pipe of tobacco*, and have a game at cards with some *blokes at home* with me, I should say, if there were any flats present, "Splodger, will you have a *Jack-surpass* of *finger-and-thumb*, and blow your yard of *tripe* of nosey me *knacker*, and have a touch of the *broads* with me and the other heaps of *coke* at my *drum*."

to provide a refuge for the nation's neediest. Ironically, under the Poor Law of 1834 these grim asylums, England's official source of government aid, became widely feared and avoided. Some people, like Dickens's Betty Higden in *Our Mutual Friend*, saw them as a fate worse than death. "Kill me sooner than take me," she cries to her visitors. "Throw this pretty child under cart-horses' feet and a loaded waggon, sooner than take him there."[56]

Her plea was justified; many people suffered and died in the workhouse since the routine was almost as restricted and austere as prison life. Upon entering, inmates were given uniforms and put to work for long hours, breaking stones or picking oakum—shredding tar-saturated ships' ropes into pieces small enough to caulk ships' timbers—labor commonly assigned to prisoners. After hours of such work, they were rewarded with a small amount of food of the poorest quality. Most inmates soon stood on the brink of starvation if they had not been in such a debilitated condition before.

Under the watchful eye of ruthless inspectors, every infraction of the rules was

The workhouse, created to improve the lives of England's poor, did just the opposite—inmates were separated from their families, worked long hours, and nearly starved.

Orphans in the workhouse were sent out as apprentices. Children working under these circumstances, such as these young shoemakers in London, were often overworked and abused by their employers.

punished. Even disobedient children were severely beaten with birch rods or shut into the "dead room" (mortuary) for the night. No one could leave the workhouse without permission; families who entered together were separated and allowed to see each other only after long intervals; and food and gifts from the outside were confiscated. Since openhanded welfare was not a policy, orphans such as Dickens's Oliver Twist were sent out to earn their living, apprenticed as chimney sweeps, domestic servants, and shop assistants. Their new masters undoubtedly took advantage of their youth and powerlessness since the orphans had no one to whom they could protest if they were overworked or abused.

Penny Gaffs and Gin Palaces

Confined by their poverty, the lower class had few opportunities to escape the drudgery that characterized their lives. Churches and street missions offered sanctuary and salvation, but religion held little attraction for the poor, since they associated it with the middle class whom they envied. According to a survey in 1851, only one out of five of the very poor attended church; Dickens wrote about this lack of interest in *Hard Times*.

> It was very strange to walk through the streets on a Sunday morning, and note how few of *them* the barbarous jangling of bells . . . called away from their own quarter, from their own close rooms, from the corners of their own streets, where they lounged listlessly, gazing at all the church and chapel going, as at a thing with which they had no manner of concern.[57]

More popular pastimes included occasional performances by street artists and traveling carnival shows that set up in vacant lots and courtyards. Music halls featuring singers and musicians were also appreciated, as were the "penny gaffs," cheap theaters that were sometimes located in a warehouse or converted shop in the neighborhood. There performers sang and put on up to five shows per day for lively crowds. The penny gaffs were notorious for their obscenity and for the promiscuous habits of the audience, and reformers continually appealed to the authorities to close them down.

Most popular in the drab inner-city surroundings were the neighborhood gin palaces, with their glittering plate glass windows, shiny gas lamps, and air of warmth and camaraderie. Inside, for a penny or two, patrons could escape the cold, chat with friends, and forget their troubles for an evening. They could choose from a variety of "wholesome" mixed drinks, usually containing gin, with col-

orful names such as "The Real Knock-Me-Down," "The Out and Out," "The No Mistake", and "The Cream of the Valley." Beer heated and mixed with gin and spices, dubbed Dog's Nose, Flip, and Purl, was also a popular drink.

Not surprisingly, reformers condemned this type of entertainment as well, calling it a waste of hard-earned money and pointing out the high rate of alcoholism among the poor. Dickens responded by going to the root of the problem. He blamed city officials for passing laws that kept the worker on the job six days a week and left him too tired and too poor to get away from such unwholesome pastimes. In *Little Dorrit*, he writes:

> Nothing to see, . . . nothing to breathe but streets, streets, streets. Nothing to

Drinking was a popular pastime in London, especially among the poor, for whom alcohol was a cheap, easily available form of entertainment and a respite from their worries.

London's Crystal Palace, built in 1851, was a glass building through which the public could walk and observe thousands of exhibits.

change the brooding mind, or raise it up. Nothing for the spent toiler to do, but to compare the monotony of his seventh day with the monotony of his six days, think what a weary life he led, and make the best of it.[58]

"Beacons of the Future"

Despite the dissimilar opportunities available to the rich and poor, some pastimes were open to those from every class. Thousands enjoyed public entertainment such as Astley's Amphitheater, with its clowns, acrobats, and orchestras; Vauxhall Gardens, famous for their fountains and fireworks; and the spectacular Crystal Palace, a stupendous glass building built in 1851, designed to hold over nineteen thousand exhibits, which varied from the Koh-i-Noor diamond to a knife with three hundred blades. Over 6 million people visited this "galaxy of splendour," as it was called. Queen Victoria enjoyed it forty-two times, Dickens only twice.

Reading was also a common form of entertainment, and anyone who could read enjoyed Dickens's novels. This simple pleasure was not open to everyone, however; there were few schools in the slums, and illiterate parents usually reared illiterate children.

Schools, particularly the concept of mandatory education, were seen by Victorians such as author Sir Arthur Conan Doyle and his renowned sleuth Sherlock Holmes as the solution to many of the country's social ills. "Light-houses, my boy! Beacons of the future! Capsules, with hundreds of bright little seeds in each, out of which will spring the wiser, better England of the future."[59] Despite such optimism, however, it would take years before the harsh and unequal education system of the nineteenth century gave way to a more enlightened approach to learning.

CHAPTER 4

Too Knocked About to Learn

In Dickens's day, education was both a luxury and a sign of gentility. The upper class was well educated. The middle class made the attempt, particularly those who had recently made their fortune in industry and understood that attendance at a good public school and university was the key to social advancement for their sons. Dickens himself sent his son Henry to Cambridge University, despite the heavy expenses involved. "I can't get my hat on in consequence of the extent to which my hair stands on end at the costs and charges of these boys,"[60] he complained. For the poor, however, schools took second place to survival. Latin, Greek, and classical history seemed a waste of time when destitution and death lurked just around the corner.

Dickens's Education

As members of the genteel middle class, Dickens's parents could not afford to send their son to the most prestigious English schools, but those he attended were respectable establishments—Mr. Giles's academy in Chatham and Mr. Jones's Wellington House, a "Classical and Commercial Academy" in London. Although Jones was quick to cane his students for breaking the rules, Dickens wrote approvingly of some of his teachers, including a "brisk little French master," a "fat little dancing master who taught the horn-pipes," and a "colourless, doubled-up, near-sighted and lame" Latin master, who tried hard to instill a desire to learn in his pupils.[61]

Dickens's educational experience was positive, but early in his life he became aware of the shortcomings of England's education system. Too many nineteenth-century schools, even those patronized by the wealthy, were inflexible, close-minded institutions, notorious for incompetence and neglect, and the author repeatedly called public attention to their faults in his letters, articles, and novels.

Charles Dickens valued education. He enjoyed the few years of schooling his parents could afford for him and later sent his own son to Cambridge University.

Public Schools

The most select public schools in England—among them Eton and Harrow—were in reality private schools that were attended by sons of the wealthy upper class. At these all-male establishments, which provided the best curricula and the most qualified instructors, boys boarded for most of the year while they concentrated on Latin, mathematics, and the classics.

Students' academic progress was carefully guided at these schools, but boys were largely unsupervised outside the classroom, since educators believed that peer pressure was a stronger influence for good conduct than adult supervision. In fact, the opposite was true. Gambling, drinking, bullying, and abuse reigned unchecked at many schools, turning the lives of some students into a living nightmare. Because of these abuses, many careful parents chose to spare their sons the ordeal and educate them at home. Some, however, continued to send their sons to public schools, believing them to be the perfect prelude to a higher education at Oxford or Cambridge University.

"Christian Gentlemen"

In 1827, Thomas Arnold became headmaster of Rugby, another popular public school in central England, and initiated much-needed improvements there. While encouraging diligence and independence, Arnold emphasized self-discipline, good behavior, and respect for others, and encouraged his charges to become "Christian gentlemen" who set good examples for those around them. His philosophy had great impact on other institutions, especially after it was popularized by writers such as Thomas Hughes, one of Arnold's pupils. In Hughes's novel *Tom Brown's Schooldays*, published in 1857, Tom's words reflect the effect of Arnold's reforms. "I want to carry away just as much Latin and Greek as will take me through Oxford respectably . . . (and) I want to leave behind me . . . the name of a fellow who never bullied a little boy or turned his back on a big one."[62]

Proper Young Ladies

Public schools were options for sons of wealthy Englishmen, but daughters were most often educated at home where they could be chaperoned and protected from evil influences. Under the guidance of a mother or a governess, most young ladies learned to sing, play the harp or piano, and sketch and paint, since these accomplishments were essential to any woman of culture and refinement. Some also opted to study foreign languages, history, geography, and mathematics.

A few select girls' academies, or finishing schools, did exist at the time, but they were uncommon. Some of the finest were located in London, and young women from all over the country were sent there to learn deportment and the fine arts. More academic London institutions included F. D. Maurice's Queens College, founded in 1848; Elizabeth Jesser Reid's Bedford College, established in 1849; and the Royal Holloway College, opened by Queen Victoria in 1886. As late as 1860, however, fewer than one thousand girls in all of London attended school outside their homes.

"Mimic Etons at Popular Prices"

Unlike the upper classes, many working-class parents had no time or money to spare on

An 1868 illustration shows girls embroidering in school. Education for upper-class girls usually meant learning proper conduct and the arts, studied at home or, less frequently, in academies.

education, preferring their children to follow in their own untutored footsteps. A growing number of the newly prosperous middle class, however, enrolled their sons in the best schools they could afford, and by the mid-1800s historic schools such as Eton, Harrow, and Rugby were overcrowded. As a result, several new institutions of learning sprang up across the country. The first were Marlborough, Cheltenham, Radley, and Lancing, followed shortly by Wellington, Clifton, and others. The best of these schools, nicknamed "mimic Etons at popular prices,"[63] were characterized by snobbery and exclusiveness, just as were more prestigious institutions of the time.

Villainous Educators

Some middle-class schools—the most notorious being those located in Yorkshire—were little more than child reformatories, marked by cruelty and deprivation, and making only a pretense at education. Dickens created such an institution for his novel *Nicholas Nickleby* after touring a northern boarding school and seeing firsthand the overcrowding and neglect there.

Dickens's fictional school was called Dotheboys Hall, a "dreary house" with "wild country round, covered with snow." Its headmaster, Mr. Squeers, was a man as vicious as he was unattractive. "He had but one eye, and the popular prejudice runs in favour of two. . . . The blank side of his face was much wrinkled and puckered up, which gave him a very sinister appearance, especially when he smiled, at which times his expression bordered closely on the villainous."[64] At Dotheboys Hall, boys were made to wash windows and clean stables as lessons in "practical philosophy," were caned if their parents failed to pay tuition, and were dosed with sulfur and molasses to cut their appetites as well as the school's food bills.

Reality was almost as black as Dickens's fiction. Many Victorian boys were sent to boarding schools where they were threatened, starved, and beaten. Some died from the neglect they suffered. Students' complaints went almost unheard since administrators censored mail and scheduled few vacations, and parents often viewed such complaints as childish exaggerations. Even the death of a student drew little attention, since mortality rates were high in those days, and the loss of a child, though tragic, was almost taken for granted by many.

Numerous schools throughout England were wretched and poorly staffed, and headmaster Squeers was only one of many villainous educators Dickens created. In *David Copperfield*, he presents Mr. Creakle, "an incapable brute, who had no more right to be possessed of the great trust he held than to be Lord High Admiral." Referring to Mr. Creakle's pupils, the young hero of that novel observes, "They were too much troubled and knocked about to learn . . . in a life of constant misfortune, torment, and worry."[65]

In *Dombey and Sons*, the head of the charity school also beats his students and is described as "a superannuated [old-fashioned] old Grinder of savage disposition, who had been appointed schoolmaster because he

Mr. Squeers, the headmaster of Dotheboys Hall in Nicholas Nickleby. *Dickens based the character on the unqualified and abusive teachers he observed in England's schools.*

didn't know anything and wasn't fit for anything."[66] In *Hard Times*, Mr. M'Choakumchild is boring and dry as dust, interested only in cramming as many facts into his pupils as possible. He represented a program, set up in 1846, that aimed to improve teacher training and better educate students. But, in fact, many teachers lacked proficiency, standards were low, and rote memorization rather than true understanding proved to be the norm.

Schoolboy Affections

Although schoolboys were expected to learn under the most trying of conditions—cold, hunger, and physical abuse—they did not always bear their pain in a stoic manner. Unlike their more reserved counterparts today, they cried openly when expressing remorse, when parting from a friend, or, as Dickens illustrates in *Nicholas Nickleby*, when meeting with an unexpected kindness. "If [Nicholas] had struck the drudge, he would have slunk away without a word. But, now, he burst into tears. 'Oh dear, oh dear!' he cried, covering his face with his cracked and horny [calloused] hands. 'My heart will break. It will, it will.'"[67]

Schoolboys embraced each other to express affection, and threw themselves on the ground or clasped their master's knees as they begged for mercy. Educators were less reserved as well, and relationships between a popular teacher and his pupils were often close enough to be considered improper in today's more cautious world.

Effective Education

Despite his quest to expose abuses in education, Dickens did write about good schools.

One such instance occurs in *David Copperfield*, when the hero recounts his days at Canterbury Academy, a school run by Doctor Strong, an amiable, intelligent headmaster who brought out the best in his pupils. "The Doctor himself was the idol of the whole school; and it must have been a badly composed school if he had been anything else, for he was the kindest of men."[68]

Undoubtedly there were many such effective institutions throughout the country. Dickens himself recommended to a friend one school in north London, founded by reformer Rowland Hill, in which "every means of study and recreation and every inducement to self-reliance and self-exertion . . . can easily be imagined."[69] Day schools also existed for children, who learned reading, mathematics, and Latin during long days of study and were free to return to their families at night.

Commercial academies were popular with tradespeople who had no money to waste on a classical education but wanted their children to master a clear, easy-to-read style of handwriting and learn enough math to be able to keep account of finances when they later took over the family business.

Limited Opportunities

Like their mothers before them, many middle-class girls received no education, instead spending their youth at home learning how to sew, clean, cook, manage a house, and raise children. Upper-middle-class families sometimes hired a governess to instruct their daughters in foreign languages, music, and art. For those who valued learning, this system worked well, as the journal of nineteen-

Educational opportunities for boys included studying classical subjects at boarding or day schools and learning basic business skills at commercial academies.

Dickens never attended the mean and miserable schools he wrote of in his novels, but with his creation of Mr. Creakle in *David Copperfield*, he captures the essence of the harsh and unqualified individuals who were part of the education system in Victorian times.

"I heard all kinds of things about the school and all belonging to it. I heard that Mr. Creakle had not preferred his claim to being a Tartar without reason; that he was the sternest and most severe of masters; that he laid about him, right and left, every day of his life, charging in among the boys like a trooper, and slashing away, unmercifully. That he knew nothing himself, but the art of slashing, being more ignorant . . . than the lowest boy in the school; that he had been, a good many years ago, a small hop-dealer in the Borough, and had taken to the schooling business after being bankrupt in hops, and making away with Mrs. Creakle's money. . . .

I heard that the man with the wooden leg, whose name was Tungay, was an obstinate barbarian who had formerly assisted in the hop business, but had come into the scholastic line with Mr. Creakle, in consequence, as was supposed among the boys, of his having broken his leg in Mr. Creakle's service. . . . I heard that with the single exception of Mr. Creakle, Tungay considered the whole establishment, masters and boys, as his natural enemies, and that the only delight of his life was to be sour and malicious."

year-old Emily Shore, who died of tuberculosis in 1839, confirms.

I cannot bear the idea of living, even in sickness, without systematically acquiring knowledge. So I shall devote myself at present to making myself mistress of history, chronology, and geography; the study of languages, mathematics, arithmetic, and the science of mechanics, etc., I must leave till I am quite restored to health.[70]

Most young women were indifferent students, however, a fortunate fact since their governesses were often only moderately educated themselves. Many governesses were widowed or unmarried gentlewomen who had fallen on hard times, and whose methods of instruction were as weak as their qualifications. Dickens created such a character in *Little Dorrit*.

Mrs. General had no opinions. Her way of forming a mind was to prevent it from forming opinions. . . . Another of her ways of forming a mind [was] to cram all articles of difficulty into cupboards, lock them up, and say they had no existence. It was the easiest way, and, beyond all comparison, the properest.[71]

Miss Monflathers, who runs a "Boarding and Day Establishment" in Dickens's *Old Curiosity Shop*, is equally close-minded. She emphasizes decorum, fancy needlework, and painting on velvet, believes the lower class is fit for nothing but factory and farm work, and carries propriety to an absurd level. "Miss Monflathers' parlour-maid inspected all visitors before admitting them; for nothing in the shape of a man, no, not even a milk man, was suffered . . . to pass that gate."[72]

Doctor Strong's Boys

Despite the existence of poor schools, fine institutions of learning did exist in Dickens's time. He creates such an establishment in *David Copperfield*, and gives it a headmaster who is both a gentleman and a scholar.

"The schoolroom was a pretty large hall, on the quietest side of the house, confronted by the stately stare of some half-dozen of the great urns, and commanding a peep of an old secluded garden belonging to the Doctor, where the peaches were ripening on the sunny south wall. . . . About five-and-twenty boys were studiously engaged at their books when we went in, but they rose to give the Doctor good morning and remained standing when they saw Mr. Wickfield and me. . . .

Doctor Strong's was an excellent school; as different from Mr. Creakle's as good is from evil. It was very gravely and decorously ordered and on a sound system; with an appeal, in everything, to the honor and good faith of the boys, and an avowed intention to rely on their possession of those qualities until they proved themselves unworthy of it, which worked wonders. . . . We had noble games out of hours, and plenty of liberty; but even then, as I remember, we were well spoken of in the town, and rarely did any disgrace, by our appearance or manner, to the reputation of Doctor Strong and Doctor Strong's boys."

Dame Schools and Ragged Schools

While increasing numbers of upper- and middle-class children went to school in Dickens's time, the majority of the poor remained uneducated. Private schools were too expensive, and free or charitable public schools, if they existed, sometimes excluded the neediest pupils because of their "rude habits, filthy condition and their want of shoes and stockings."[73] Those youngsters who were allowed to enroll received lessons in reading, writing, and spelling, as well as regular lectures on the benefits of religion, hard work, and humility. The disillusioned son of one farm laborer recited a common maxim: "Boys and girls must never 'pick and steal', nor lie, nor have any envy of folk luckier than themselves; they must learn to labour truly to get their own living and order themselves lowly and reverently to their betters."[74]

At times the educational needs of a village or neighborhood were met by an impoverished female who set up a dame school in her home. There, for a small sum, she would often instruct a few children in the basics of reading and arithmetic, although such efforts were often woefully inadequate, as Dickens describes in *Great Expectations*.

Mr. Wopsle's great-aunt kept an evening school in the village; that is to say, she was a ridiculous old woman of limited means and unlimited infirmity who used to go to sleep from six to seven every evening in the society of youth who paid twopence per week each for the improving opportunity of seeing her do it.[75]

To combat such widespread neglect, in 1844 philanthropist Lord Shaftesbury helped establish the Ragged School Union, designed specifically to provide education for the poor. Under its auspices, free grammar schools were set up to help educate the poor, although curricula remained religiously oriented, too boring to hold the attention of many students who were used to the freedom of the streets. Despite these drawbacks, by 1846 twenty-six ragged schools were operating in London, teaching over two thousand pupils.

Obstacles to Learning

Even the most dedicated of the poor regularly encountered serious obstacles to learning, and school attendance averaged less than two years for most children. Malnutrition, illness, and abuse weakened their ability to concentrate, especially when educators emphasized memo-

rization and rote learning rather than a more creative approach. Student-teacher ratios were high, so no child received personal attention. In at least one school, a single teacher was in charge of two hundred or more boys.

Lack of parental support was a handicap, as well. According to one report, parents were "too indifferent, or too ignorant, or too vicious, or too little able to command their children, ever to avail themselves of such educational opportunities as existed."[76] In *Great Expectations*, kindhearted Joe Gargery explains to Pip how his father's alcoholism hampered his own schooling.

My mother and me we ran away from my father several times; and then . . . she'd

Public schools for poor children drilled messages of moral and pious behavior into their students and stressed rote memorization.

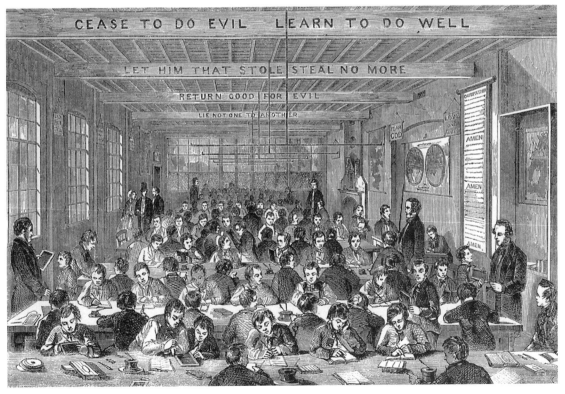

Although Dickens found fault with ragged schools, he admitted they were a first step toward public education for all children. Dickens describes a visit to one such school in a letter to the *Daily News*, a London publication, on February 4, 1846. The letter is part of *Selected Letters of Charles Dickens*, edited by David Paroissien.

"[The school] consisted at that time of either two or three—I forget which—miserable rooms, upstairs in a miserable house. . . .

The close, low, chamber at the back, in which the boys were crowded, was so foul and stifling as to be, at first, almost insupportable. . . . Huddled together on a bench about the room . . . were a crowd of boys, varying from mere infants to young men; sellers of fruit, herbs, lucifer-matches, flints; sleepers under the dry arches of bridges; young thieves and beggars—with nothing natural to youth about them: with nothing frank, ingenuous, or pleasant in their faces; low-browed, vicious, cunning, wicked; abandoned of all help but this; speeding downward to destruction. . . .

This was the Class I saw at the Ragged School. They could not be trusted with books; they could only be instructed orally; they were difficult of reduction to anything like attention, obedience, or decent behaviour. . . . Yet, even here . . . something had been done already. The Ragged School . . . had inculcated some association with the name of the Almighty, which was not an oath: and had taught them to look forward in a hymn . . . to another life, which would correct the miseries and woes of this."

say, 'now, please God, you shall have some schooling child'. . . . But my father . . . couldn't a-bear to be without us. . . . He'd come . . . and make such a row. . . . And then he took us home and hammered us. Which you see, Pip, . . . were a drawback on my learning.[77]

Pathway to Crime

Without education and a good job to promote success and security, many of the poor turned to crime to survive. As reformers discovered, however, breaking the law was more than a survival tactic. It was a way to "even the score" with those who were well-to-do. Victorian clergyman James Greenwood explained: "[The poor] have an ingrained conviction that it is *you* who are wrong . . . in appropriating all the good things the world affords, leaving none for them but what they steal. . . . They believe honest people are their bitterest enemies."[78]

This rationale, generated by the enormous gaps that existed between the haves and have-nots in Victorian England, motivated many of the poor to embrace a life of crime despite the best efforts of those who worked to give them better lives.

Palaces of Retribution

Crime was widespread in Victorian England, especially in London, where law enforcement was often disorganized and inadequate, and criminals had little to lose and much to gain by breaking the law. For many, life was already a cruel punishment. When alcoholism, anger, and despair were added to destitution, it was small wonder that more Victorians did not turn to crime.

Pickpockets and Resurrection Men

Every type of vice and violation occurred in nineteenth-century England, from relatively minor infractions such as vagrancy, disorderly conduct, and begging to serious offenses such as child abuse, drunkenness, gang attacks, and mass murder. Petty theft, burglary, purse snatching, and domestic abuse were common crimes, but so were extortion, counterfeiting, and embezzlement. Pickpockets practiced their art in broad daylight and were hard to deter since they were quick, cunning, and highly skilled. Many were children who eluded capture by slipping away and then sprinting for cover. Others were adults who worked in teams, assumed the appearance of tradespeople or businessmen, and were careful to blend with the crowd after pocketing their loot.

Lawbreakers who specialized in particular crimes were described in the vernacular of the streets. "Magsmen" conned and robbed country visitors who were inexperienced in city ways. "Smashers" passed counterfeit money. "Screwsmen" specialized in keys and safe breaking. "Resurrection men," such as Jerry Cruncher in Dickens's *Tale of Two Cities*, unearthed newly buried bodies from graveyards, robbed them, and sometimes sold them to medical schools for research purposes.

"Chirrupers" earned their name by extorting money from music hall entertainers, threatening to disrupt performances if they were not well paid. Those practicing the "kinchin lay" stole only from small children, since these young victims were numerous, defenseless, and often on the streets. One woman served six months hard labor for stealing fourteen pairs of boots from various children whom she waylaid as they ran errands for parents and employers.

Walking the Streets

Theft was not the only crime that women committed. Historian Roy Porter writes, "Prostitution flaunted itself in Victorian London,"[79] and such was the case; in 1859, there were an estimated eighty thousand prostitutes in the city, most of them emaciated and dirty, some preteens who were already the mistresses of men in their slum neighborhoods. They walked the streets boldly since police were bribed to ignore them or were busy with more serious offenses. Even without this safeguard, however, most were willing to risk arrest and a fine

A newspaper article describes one of Jack the Ripper's murders. Jack the Ripper's 1888 killing spree was a chilling example of the violence and danger London prostitutes faced.

Bloody Death

Jack the Ripper did not terrorize Londoners until after Dickens's time, but there were other spectacular murders that caught public attention earlier in the century. In 1811 the Ratcliffe Highway murders involved the bloody deaths of seven people, including a child, a young servant girl, and an elderly couple. The age of the victims, as well as the heinousness of the crime, turned public opinion against the killer, a sailor named Williams, who hanged himself before he could come to trial. After his death, Williams's body was reportedly carted through the streets, then buried in an obscure grave with a stake driven through its heart.

During Dickens's early adulthood, the Bethnal Green murders, involving a gang of body snatchers who sometimes provided their own corpses by killing homeless orphans, produced much sensation and outrage. Another case involved a woman named Eliza Ross, who enticed young women to her home and killed them for their clothes, disposing of their remains on dustheaps in her neighborhood. According to Millicent Rose, Ross was "addicted to drink and so heartless that she thought nothing of wearing a dead girl's bonnet for months after the wretched creature's disappearance."[81]

because they could earn more in one night than in a whole week of sweatshop labor.

Despite its monetary advantages, the physical cost of such a career was high. Sexually transmitted diseases and tuberculosis were rampant and incurable. Violence was a fact of life, and despair drove many to suicide, as Nancy acknowledges just before she is beaten to death in Dickens's *Oliver Twist*. "Look at that dark water. How many times do you read of such as I who spring into the tide, and leave no living thing, to care for, or bewail them."[80]

In late summer and fall of 1888, women like Nancy lived in greater than normal fear as Jack the Ripper prowled the alleyways of London, slitting the throats of at least five prostitutes before his killing spree mysteriously ended.

Dredgermen and Corpse Collectors

While Eliza Ross disposed of her victims on dustheaps, other criminals preferred the Thames River when it came to getting rid of a body. In fact, all kinds of crime went on near the river, particularly in the shadow of the London docks, where a fortune in goods beckoned and the comings and goings of ships and workers increased the difficulty of detecting crime and tracking down suspects.

Ships and barges were easy targets for thieves, since they could be boarded from all sides and offered many hiding places. Watchmen were notoriously underpaid and could be bribed to ignore any suspicious activity. Night was a favorite time for robbers to strike. Tier-rangers (who stole personal articles from the crew) and dredgermen (who threw articles overboard and dredged them out of the water later) worked best under cover of darkness, when the docks were deserted and the crew slept. Corpse collectors, who sold the bodies of those who drowned (after first ransacking their pockets for valuables), also preferred carrying on their gruesome tasks at night.

Daytime theft was all too common, however. Stevedores, or lumpers, hired to unload cargo were not above stealing from their employers, as one Victorian observed.

Many of them were provided with an under dress, denominated a *Jemmey*, with pockets before and behind: also with long narrow bags or pouches, which, when filled, were lashed to their legs and thighs, and concealed under wide trousers.—By these means they were enabled to carry off sugars, coffee, cocoa, ginger, pimento and every other article.[82]

Young Delinquents

In London's rookeries, even the most honest parent found it impossible to wholly protect their offspring from dishonest influences, and many children learned early in their lives that wrongdoing could pay if one was careful and clever.

Willingly or unwillingly, children participated in many illicit activities that ranged from picking pockets to prostitution. Children stole laundry and pawned it, rolled (robbed) drunks, and created diversions for other criminals. The most agile were valued as "snakesmen"—individuals who could slip through small openings such as windows and vents to aid in a burglary. Bill Sikes recognized undersized Oliver's potential for such work in *Oliver Twist*. "The aperture was so small, that the inmates had probably not thought it worth while to defend . . . but it was large enough to admit a boy of Oliver's size."[83]

Children like Oliver who had no family to protect them were particularly vulnerable to corrupting influences, as Victorian clergyman James Greenwood explained in 1869. "In every low criminal neighbourhood there are numbers of children who never knew their parents, and who are fed and clothed by the old thieves, and made to earn their wages by dishonest practices."[84] Dickens also called attention to professional thief trainers in *Oliver Twist*, creating the character of Fagin, who tries to lure Oliver into the gang of boys he has carefully trained.

The old man would tell them stories of robberies he had committed in his younger days: mixed up with so much that was droll and curious, that Oliver could not help laughing heartily. . . . In short, the wily old [man] had the boy in his toils; and . . . was now slowly instilling into his soul the poison which he hoped would blacken it, and change its hue forever.[85]

Although Oliver is redeemed, most dishonest youngsters were soon turned into daring and hardened criminals, almost impossible to reform since they had never been taught the difference between right and wrong and had an ingrained distrust of honest people.

Bobbies

As crime in London increased in the early nineteenth century, time-honored law enforcement systems that relied on the efforts of unarmed constables, beadles (minor parish officials), and night watchmen became inadequate defenses. Changes made during Dickens's lifetime helped improve the system, however. In 1829, England's Home Secretary Sir Robert Peel created the Metropolitan Police, an agency with authority to oversee virtually all of London. Unlike the city's earlier protectors, Peel's policemen were carefully chosen and trained, and were equipped with heavy wooden clubs.

Many Londoners were suspicious of such an organized, centralized force and feared that the new agency would soon become an oppressive tool of the government, but the "Bobbies," or "Peelers" (named after their creator), were "civil and attentive to all persons, of every rank and class."[86] They soon won the approval of most law-abiding citizens, and their presence slowed the increase in crime as lawbreakers came to realize that their chances of escaping capture had lessened.

A scene from Oliver Twist *shows Oliver running from a crowd shouting, "Stop thief!" Like Oliver, children in rookeries learned theft and other crimes from more experienced criminals.*

Sir Robert Peel created the Metropolitan Police in 1829. His "Bobbies," or "Peelers," earned the respect of most Londoners and slowed the city's escalating crime rate.

Minor Crimes, Stiff Penalties

For those who were caught breaking the law, punishment was often a term of imprisonment. Men, women, and children as young as twelve could be sentenced to a month of hard labor for a crime as petty as stealing rabbits. Henry Mayhew noted that, in 1851, almost half of the population in Coldbath Fields House of Correction were there because they could not pay fines for infractions such as obstructing traffic or public drunkenness. Wealth had its privileges, however; vandalism and other minor misdeeds that would land poor boys in jail were often brushed aside as pranks and harmless fun when the sons of the upper class were involved.

Prison was so much a part of life that Dickens used it in *Little Dorrit* as a symbol of the poverty, narrow-mindedness, and government red tape that fettered Victorian society. Those unfortunate enough to be incarcerated were often locked up with no consideration given to age, sex, or crime. When Dickens visited Newgate in 1835, he observed

> five-and-twenty or thirty prisoners, all under sentence of death . . . men of all ages and appearance, from a hardened old offender with swarthy face and grizzly beard . . . to a handsome boy, not fourteen years old . . . who had been condemned for burglary.[87]

In some facilities, a section of the building was set aside for debtors, felons awaiting trial, and minor offenders, with hardened criminals housed separately. Prisons such as Newgate were eventually reserved for the worse offenders.

With few exceptions, conditions in these institutions were squalid, brutal, and restrictive. Such severity was designed to discourage future offenses and encourage respectable citizens to remain honest. Rather than stern reminders, however, prisons actually inspired hatred and rebellion, and served as training grounds for young offenders who learned the secrets of the business from more experienced offenders and from one another. Henry Mayhew writes, "True, the place is called a house of correction; but, rightly viewed, it is simply a criminal preparatory school."[88]

"Remember the Poor Debtors"

Imprisonment for debt was such a common practice in Victorian England that so-called debtors' prisons were set aside to house offenders. King's Bench, the Fleet, and the Marshalsea were the best known in London. Since

In *Oliver Twist*, Dickens paints a colorful picture of the training street urchins received at the hands of master thieves during early Victorian times. In this scene, Fagin (the merry old gentleman), the Artful Dodger, and Charley Bates show Oliver the ins and outs of successfully picking pockets.

"When the breakfast was cleared away, the merry old gentleman and the two boys played at a very curious and uncommon game, which was performed in this way: The merry old gentleman: placing a snuff-box in one pocket of his trousers, a note-case in the other, and a watch in his waistcoat-pocket: with a guard-chain round his neck: and sticking a mock diamond pin in his shirt: buttoned his coat tight round him, and putting his spectacle-case and handkerchief in his pockets, trotted up and down the room . . . in imitation of the manner in which old gentlemen walk about the streets any hour in the day. Sometimes he stopped at the fire-place, and sometimes at the door; making belief that he was staring with all his might into shop-windows. . . . All this time, the two boys followed him closely about: getting out of his sight, so nimbly, every time he turned around, that it was impossible to follow their motions. At last, the Dodger trod upon his toes . . .

The Artful Dodger from Oliver Twist *was a master pickpocket and member of a gang of young thieves.*

while Charley Bates stumbled up against him behind; and in that one moment they took from him . . . snuff-box, note-case, watch, guard-chain, shirt-pin, pocket-handkerchief; even the spectacle-case. If the old gentleman felt a hand in any one of his pockets, he cried out where it was; and then the game began all over again."

men who were in prison for debt often had wives and children to support, families were allowed to move into the prison and live, rent free, until such time as the head of the house settled with his creditors and was released.

Prison terms could be lengthy and demoralizing, as Dickens illustrates in *Little Dorrit*, the story of a young girl who is born and raised in Marshalsea Prison, where her father has been held for years. The most unfortunate inmates were often driven to pawn their clothes to buy food and lived crowded together with other families in small, foul-smelling cells where many became ill with typhus, dysentery, and scurvy. To help the most wretched survive, officials of some prisons created a beggars' grate overlooking a public street. Dickens describes one in *The Pickwick*

Papers. "There was a kind of iron cage in the wall of the Fleet Prison, within which was posted some man of hungry looks, who, from time to time, rattled a money-box, and exclaimed in a mournful voice, 'Pray remember the poor debtors; pray, remember the poor debtors.'" [89] In some locales, passersby were surprisingly generous. At the Rochester city jail one keeper remarked, "[The] liberality of the public is so great that we cannot keep the prisoners sober." [90]

Corruption

A variation of debtors' prison was the "spunging house," where well-to-do spendthrifts were temporarily held until their families paid their debts. Occupants, who included members of the upper class, passed the time in relative luxury, eating well, visiting with friends, playing cards, and drinking wine in the evenings.

Money talked in Dickens's time, particularly in cases involving less desperate criminals. Turnkeys were easily bribed, and if a man was lucky he could obtain many of the comforts of home. Mr. Pickwick, who goes to Fleet Prison for breach of promise in *The Pickwick Papers*, soon escapes the noise and drunkenness he first encounters and is able to obtain a "capital room" complete with carpet, a table and bed, a teakettle, and regular supplies of beer and wine. Dickens's friend Leigh Hunt, who was imprisoned for libel at Horsemonger Prison in London, decorated his large cell with rose-patterned wallpaper, flowers, and a piano, inspiring his friends to describe it as "a fragment of fairyland." [91] Some inmates bought the right to leave prison during the day, while others served their term "within the rules"—that is, living anywhere within two and a half miles of the prison.

Newgate

Historic prisons such as London's notorious Newgate, which had housed prisoners since the twelfth century, offered none of the benefits enjoyed by Mr. Pickwick and Leigh Hunt. Newgate originally held criminals guilty of all kinds of offenses; after 1847, however, only those awaiting trial at the nearby Old Bailey criminal court were housed there. Dickens, who visited Newgate in 1835, called it a "gloomy depository of the guilt and misery of London." [92]

Inside this much-feared palace of retribution, inmates were confined in bare, often overcrowded, wards where little light or fresh air came in through narrow barred windows.

Rows of inmates are stacked on top of each other in this illustration of the sick men's ward at Marshalsea Prison. Disease was common in prisons, where sanitation and health care were severely lacking.

Stone walls and floors were continually cold and damp. Exercise was held to a minimum, food was poor, and many deaths occurred from disease and poor nutrition.

In earlier times, prisoners at Newgate had been herded together, regardless of age or offense, into filthy cells where all kinds of evil and abuse went unnoticed by prison guards, and where obvious infractions were punished by shackling or whipping. By 1813, however, reformer Elizabeth Fry was working to improve conditions for women prisoners, and by Dickens's visit, typhus epidemics were curbed, offenders were segregated according to their sex and crime, and those awaiting execution no longer had to endure torments such as being forced to sit beside their own coffins while attending chapel. Despite improvements, however, Newgate remained a symbol of grim retribution to the English, and the fascinated public shivered when they passed it by, imagining unspeakable tortures going on behind its dreadful walls.

Pentonville Penitentiary

Unlike Marshalsea, Newgate, and other prisons built in an earlier age, Pentonville Penitentiary, which opened in 1842, was one of several "modern" prisons constructed in the late eighteenth and early nineteenth centuries. These were cleaner and more spacious than earlier institutions, and most followed the increasingly popular philosophy that punishment should be directed at the mind rather than the body.

At Pentonville, officials relied on silence, Scripture, and hard work to punish and reform criminals. Rather than being crowded together in cramped quarters, prisoners were isolated into small cubicles where they lived

Hard Labor

Although prisons would eventually become more humane, in Dickens's time they were designed to punish and break the spirit of offenders rather than rehabilitate them. To this end, various pointless and exhausting pastimes such as the treadmill and the crank were invented, as author Gillian Avery explains in *Victorian People*.

"The debate on how prisoners should be treated inevitably included what work they should be made to do. There were those who said they should be trained in some skill by which they could earn their living when they were freed. The harsher said no, they must be punished by performing some hard and useless labour which broke the spirit by its monotony and uselessness. To this end the treadmill and the crank were devised. The treadmill was a revolving cylinder with steps upon it. As the prisoners, each partitioned off from the next, trod up the steps so the wheel revolved. It was heavy, exhausting, much hated work, and was extensively used by prisons run on the Silent System. . . . Shot drill was another punishment that could be carried out in silence. Here the men had to stand endlessly shifting a pile of cannon balls from one side of them to the other and then back again. Crank labour . . . could be carried out in the isolation of the cell. A handle fixed in the wall had to be turned so many thousand times a day—again to no purpose whatever."

Newgate was a more traditional correctional institution than the debtors' prisons; it housed criminals of all types and focused on punishment to break the inmates' spirits.

for months in solitary confinement, forbidden to speak and only allowed outside their cells for a brief (and solitary) period of daily exercise and religious instruction. During such outings, each wore a mask that made nonverbal communication with other prisoners virtually impossible.

In contrast to the unstructured routine of traditional prisons, life was well regulated at Pentonville, and bells marked each stage of the day's schedule. Every item that furnished a cell had its proper place, from the table against the wall to the neatly folded hammock and the corner shelf holding a bar of soap and a Bible. Food was delivered through a small trapdoor at regular intervals, and inmates worked alone in their cells at an assigned task. One letter or visit from family was permitted twice a year, and all communications were rigorously censored.

"Exemplary Punishment"

For troublemakers, discipline designed to weaken the most hardened character was imposed at Pentonville. Tortures such as cranking (turning a handle in a wall for hours on end) or the treadmill (an endless flight of steps attached to a revolving wheel) were common activities that wore down a person physically and emotionally. One official described the treadmill as "the most tiresome, distressing, exemplary punishment that has ever been contrived by human ingenuity."[93] The most incorrigible troublemakers were

An 1862 illustration shows convicts at Pentonville Prison exercising in a group, a relatively new reform by this date, but still subjected to the older policy of wearing masks on their faces.

confined to the "dark cells," cold, pitch-black holes in the depths of the prison. Three days was the prescribed length of punishment, but three week sentences were not unheard-of.

Despite its orderly routine, after weeks of isolation and deprivation at Pentonville, prisoners sometimes went insane from depression and loneliness. Even insanity did not end their incarceration, since those who remained permanently affected were confined in an asylum, and those who recovered were sent back to prison to serve out their sentence. By 1850, however, Pentonville administrators abandoned certain features of prison life—solitary chapel cells, isolated exercise yards, and masks—motivated by the realization that strict practices were not reducing crime rates or reforming criminals.

Walk to the Gallows

Dickens recognized the need for prisons in a society plagued by crime, just as he reluctantly admitted that capital punishment was necessary to rid the world of murderers. He openly deplored the practice for its brutality and finality, however, and because it was imposed on many who did not deserve such punishment.

Early Victorian criminals were regularly sentenced to hang for offenses such as robbery, arson, and homosexuality. Two hundred twenty such offenses were on the law books early in the century; only after 1832 were laws passed abolishing the death penalty for certain kinds of theft.

For those sentenced to death, executions commonly took place in a prison yard, in full view of the public. In Dickens's *Great Expectations*, the minister of justice at Newgate gives Pip a tour of that yard in all its grim detail.

> He was so good as to . . . show me where the gallows was kept, and also where people were publicly whipped, and then he showed me the debtors' door, out of which culprits came to be hanged . . . giving me to understand that "four on 'em" would come out at that door the day after to-morrow at eight in the morning to be killed in a row.[94]

Although Dickens passionately opposed it, public execution was an accepted practice in his day, since officials believed the sight would have a sobering effect on potential lawbreakers. The opposite proved to be true, and public hangings became so popular that they drew thousands of spectators who drank, shouted insults, and reveled at the grisly sight of men and women struggling and kicking at the end of a rope before they died.

Transportation

Since so many crimes rated a prison sentence in Victorian times, the government relied on transportation (banishment) of the most serious offenders to help relieve the problem of overcrowding. The practice began in the eighteenth century, when shiploads of male and female convicts were sent to the American colonies and, after the Revolutionary War, to New South Wales in eastern Australia. The latter held the attraction of being large, unsettled, and a British territory. Between 1788 and 1868, more than 160,000 convicts were sent to Australia where they were confined to penal colonies. When the costs of such

The Horror of the Gallows

Dickens hated public executions, believing that they glamorized criminals rather than discouraging crime. He expresses his views in a letter to the *Times*, dated November 14, 1849. The letter is included in *Selected Letters of Charles Dickens*, edited by David Paroissien.

"I believe that a sight so inconceivably awful as the wickedness and levity of the immense crowd collected at that execution this morning could be imagined by no man, and could be presented in no heathen land under the sun. When I came upon the scene at midnight, the *shrillness* of the cries and howls that were raised from time to time . . . from a concourse of boys and girls already assembled in the best places, made my blood run cold. . . . When the day dawned, thieves, low prostitutes, ruffians and vagabonds of every kind, flocked on to the ground, with every variety of offensive and foul behavior. Fightings, faintings, whistlings, . . . tumultuous demonstrations of indecent delight when swooning women were dragged out of the crowd . . . gave a new zest to the general excitement. . . . When the two miserable creatures who attracted all this ghastly sight about them were turned quivering into the air, there was no more emotion, no more pity, no more thought that two immortal souls had gone to judgment . . . than if the name of Christ had never been heard in this world."

colonies became too high, the government released its convicts into the custody of anyone who would support them in exchange for their labor.

Many criminals strongly objected to being banished from their homeland into the unknown; in the 1780s, one recently sentenced woman, Sarah Mills, declared, "I would rather die than go out of my own country to be devoured by savages."[95] While no one was devoured, and a number like Abel Magwitch in Dickens's *Great Expectations* earned a new start in life, the majority of convicts sent to work in Australia were justified in their protests, since they were considered little better than slaves by their overseers.

Conditions in penal colonies, established to hold serious troublemakers and escapees, were even worse than those endured by the majority in Australia. Prisoners there were regularly tortured, starved, and set to work on chain gangs and in coal mines. Since British officials did not care if former criminals flourished or perished, no one took action to correct the hellish conditions that drove men to suicide and murder. Only after years of protests from humanitarians was the system reformed, and the practice of transporting came to an end in 1868.

The Hulks

Convicts awaiting transportation were often confined in decaying naval warships (men-of-war), which were anchored in the Thames and other rivers around the country. The idea of turning such ships into prisons came about in the late 1770s when England had to find short-term housing for prisoners it had for-

A view inside a ship carrying convicts to an Australian penal colony. In the eighteenth and nineteenth centuries, England sent its most serious criminals to these penal settlements, where conditions were even worse than in English prisons.

Hulks were created in the late 1770s to ease prison overcrowding. The ships quickly became fixtures in many of England's rivers, packed with prisoners who faced hunger, disease, violence, and death.

merly transported to America. Established prisons were already overcrowded, and the unused ships seemed like reasonable structures for temporary use. Not surprisingly, they soon became permanent fixtures, and by 1841, over three thousand prisoners languished aboard these prison vessels.

The "hulks," as they were called, were often moored near a mudflat or fog-shrouded marsh, and were viewed by the general populace as sinister edifices marked by violence and death. In *Great Expectations*, the reader sees them through the eyes of Dickens's youthful protagonist, Pip. "By the light of the torches, we saw the black Hulk lying out a little way from the mud of the shore, like a wicked Noah's ark. Cribbed and barred and moored by massive rusty chains, the prison-ship seemed in my young eyes to be ironed like the prisoners."[96]

The vessels were damp, filthy, overcrowded and disease-ridden, and prisoners were poorly fed, wore rags and chains, and performed hard labor such as digging and transporting sand to be used as ballast (stabilizing weight) in ships. Conditions were so unhealthy that one out of four died, and so dangerous that at night guards went belowdecks into prisoners' quarters only in armed parties. Most preferred to simply lock the hatches and allow fighting and abuse to reign unchecked below. Despite such appalling circumstances, however, many criminals preferred to be incarcerated in the hulks since discipline was lax and conditions in other prisons could be almost as bad.

Greater Hazards

Debate over crime and England's penal system continued throughout Dickens's lifetime, with further reforms taking place as authorities learned that pitiless, ironhanded methods were a detriment rather than a benefit to society as a whole.

The public also became aware that lawbreakers were not the only serious threat to their world. Filth, pollution, and decay were equal, if not greater, hazards, and Dickens personalized the danger for his readers when he wrote,

Into the imperfect sewers of this City [London] you have the immense mass of corruption . . . lazily thrown out of sight to rise in poisonous gases into your house at night when your sleeping children will most readily absorb them and to find its languid way at last into the river that you drink.[97]

CHAPTER

6 Dustheaps and Disease

Dickens was not exaggerating when he wrote of "the immense mass of corruption" that sickened and killed so many people in his day. England's polluted environment affected the health of every Victorian. Contamination was everywhere. Chemicals from mills and factories hung in the air and poisoned nearby rivers. Piles of garbage bred disease-carrying rats and flies. Mud and manure clogged the streets and were tracked into homes on shoes and the hems of women's skirts. In a letter to the *London Times* on July 5, 1849, fifty-four laborers expressed their concern over the danger from so much uncontrolled dirt and waste:

> We are Sur, as it may be, living in a Wilderniss, so far as the rest of London knows anything of us. . . . We live in muck and filthe. We aint got no privez [bathrooms], no dust bins, no drains, no water splies [supplies], and no drain or suer [sewer] in the whole place. The Suer Company . . . take no notice watsomedever [whatsoever] of our complaints. The Stenche of a Gully-hole is disgustin. We al of us suffer, and numbers are ill, and if the Colera comes Lord help us.[98]

Privies and Dustheaps

Safe disposal of waste was almost unheard-of in Dickens's day, and in London the rookeries were the sites of the worst filth. There, garbage was tossed into gutters, where it lay until it decayed and was washed away by the rain. With bathroom facilities nonexistent, adults discreetly made use of a back courtyard or quiet alleyway, while their less-inhibited children relieved themselves in the streets in full view of any passerby who might happen along.

Even in better neighborhoods, garbage and litter were simply swept into dustheaps and then disposed of in fields, vacant lots, or in huge rat-infested garbage dumps outside the city. Toilet facilities were commonly chamber pots and privies (pit toilets) that allowed waste to drain into cesspits and eventually leach into drinking water. As time passed a few homes had flush toilets that were connected to sewers, but until about 1850, even sewers were uncovered and carried untreated refuse directly to nearby rivers.

Streets and Slaughterhouses

Victorian streets and roads were sites of constant pollution, since they were unpaved and befouled by the manure of endless horses. In dry weather they were dusty and odoriferous, in the rainy season, muddy and slippery. In London, street sweepers helped keep the crossings clean for passersby, and on rainy days, pedestrians who could afford overshoes wore them. Despite such efforts, however, dodging between carriages and carts and around piles of horse droppings usually resulted in splashed

Garbage disposal in most neighborhoods in Victorian England meant tossing refuse out the window. The streets and alleys were also fouled with human waste and horse manure.

trousers and soiled skirts, if not worse. Dickens writes in *Bleak House*:

> [There was] as much mud in the streets, as if the waters had but newly retired from the face of the earth. . . . Dogs, undistinguishable in mire. Horses, scarcely better; splashed to their very blinkers. Foot passengers, jostling one another's umbrellas . . . and losing their foot-hold at street-corners, where tens of thousands of other foot passengers have been slipping and sliding since the day broke.[99]

Londoners took dirty streets in stride, but they were less tolerant of the city's livestock markets. Once located at the edge of town, these markets had been engulfed by the fast-growing suburbs, with the result that thousands of cattle, sheep, and goats had to be herded through urban streets and were corralled in the same vicinity as homes, schools, churches, and hospitals. The noise and smells associated with the animals themselves were offensive, but odors from related industries that grew up around the markets—slaughter yards, and plants for bone crushing, blood boiling, hide preparing, and tallow melting—were asphyxiating, especially on hot summer days. Waste from such plants drained into water supplies and served as breeding grounds for insects, vermin, and disease.

"So Foul a Source"

Along with waste that inevitably found its way into water supplies around the country, chemicals from factories were regularly flushed into England's rivers, turning them rainbow colors and killing fish and other wildlife. In *Hard Times*, Dickens writes of a fictional "black canal . . . and a river that ran purple with ill-smelling dye,"[100] using it as an example of water pollution in actual industrial centers around the country.

London was the best known of those centers. There, raw sewage, animal carcasses, and even dead bodies contaminated the Thames River, and combinations of chemicals on its surface created poisonous gases that made boaters ill. Dickens's friend the Reverend Sydney Smith remarked with considerable astuteness in 1834, "He who drinks a tumbler of London Water has literally in his stomach more animated beings than there are Men, Women and Children on the face of the Globe."[101] Another concerned Victorian, Sir Francis Burdett, petitioned the House of Commons in 1827 to stop using the Thames as a source of drinking water.

The factories where livestock was processed filled the air with a choking odor and produced waste that tainted the water supply and spread disease.

The water taken from the River Thames at Chelsea, for the use of the inhabitants of the western part of the metropolis, being charged with the contents of the great common sewers, the draining from dunghills, . . . the refuse of hospitals, slaughter houses, colour, lead and soap works, drug mills and manufactories, and with all sorts of decomposed animals and vegetable substances . . . ought no longer to be taken up by any of the water companies from so foul a source.[102]

The Menace of Disease

Poor sanitary practices led to disease and epidemics, especially in urban areas. Cholera, a deadly intestinal disease transmitted in contaminated water, swept London at least three times between 1832 and 1855. Smallpox and typhoid fever were constant menaces. Illnesses such as measles and whooping cough killed thousands of children who were too weak or malnourished to resist.

Disease usually struck hardest among the poor and lower working classes because they lived in close proximity to one another in unsanitary environs and could not easily leave their homes during an epidemic. The well-to-do, with money and leisure to travel abroad or escape to their country estates, avoided the worst exposure.

Parliament paid little attention to cholera and other epidemics until June 1858, when the Thames River became so contaminated and evil smelling that its fumes penetrated into their chambers. "The great stink," as it was called, caused panic among the members, who shared the common belief that foul odor *was* disease and was therefore deadly.

To combat the threat, tons of lime were dumped into the Thames and the windows of Parliament were hung with sheets soaked with lime (an accepted disease-preventing measure). The smell eventually faded, but the

Market Morning

As London grew, its livestock yards became intolerable to urban dwellers who had to cope with terrible odors and traffic jams when cattle were driven through the streets. In *Oliver Twist*, the villainous Bill Sikes leads Oliver through the Smithfield market as they prepare to commit a burglary.

"It was market-morning. The ground was covered, nearly ankle-deep, with filth and mire; and a thick steam, perpetually [rose] from the reeking bodies of the cattle, and [mingled] with the fog. . . . Countrymen, butchers, drovers, hawkers, boys, thieves, idlers, and vagabonds of every low grade, were mingled together in a dense mass; the whistling of drovers, the barking of dogs, the bellowing and plunging of oxen, the bleating of sheep, the grunting and squeaking of pigs; the cries of hawkers, the shouts, oaths, and quarrelling on all sides; the ringing of bells and roar of voices, that issued from every public-house; the crowding, pushing, driving, beating, whooping and yelling; the hideous and discordant din that resounded from every corner of the market; and the unwashed, unshaven, squalid, and dirty figures constantly running to and fro, and bursting in and out of the throng; rendered it a stunning and bewildering scene, which quite confounded the senses.

An 1850 cartoon is captioned, "A drop of London water." The cartoon satirizes the pollution in the Thames River, a vile mixture of sewage, chemicals, and even animal carcasses and human corpses.

incident focused public attention on water pollution, and Parliament soon passed a bill designed to improve sewers and prevent a recurrence of the problem.

"A Disc Without Rays"

As Victorians began to understand the dangers from filth and polluted water, they also began to note the harmful effects of air pollution, which was masked by fog, an integral part of the English climate.

English fogs were so heavy and oppressive that Dickens often used them to lend a menacing tone to his novels. In *Bleak House*, where fog is a symbol for the "rotten workings" of England's legal system, he writes, "Fog [was] everywhere. . . . Fog on the Essex Marshes, fog on the Kentish Heights. . . . Fog

in the eyes and throats of ancient Greenwich pensioners . . . fog in the stem and bowl of the afternoon pipe of the wrathful skipper."[103] And in *Great Expectations*:

> The marsh-mist was so thick that the wooden finger on the post directing people to our village . . . was invisible to me until I was quite close under it. . . . The mist was heavier yet when I got out upon the marshes, so that instead of my running at everything, everything seemed to run at me.[104]

Dense to begin with, England's fogs gradually became heavier and more menacing as a result of the pollutants that billowed from thousands of smokestacks and chimneys across the country. Coal was the most popular and widespread of all fuels in Victorian England, used

A photo of Sheffield, England, during the industrial revolution. In some areas, England's factories spewed forth so much soot and smog that sunlight was blocked out.

for cooking and heating homes as well as in endless numbers of businesses such as brewing, baking, glassmaking, pottery making, and blacksmithing. All of England's steam engines were powered by coal, while coke, a processed form of the fuel, was necessary for iron making.

Poisonous sulfur dioxide and ash were by-products of burning coal, and when weather conditions were right, their presence over London and manufacturing towns such as Manchester and Birmingham made air so noxious that some residents had difficulty breathing. In the worst regions, soot and smog were so thick that the sun looked like "a disc without rays,"[105] plants died from poisonous fumes that smothered them, and smog-blackened buildings dominated the landscape.

Melancholy Madness

Dickens writes of such towns in *The Old Curiosity Shop*, shrouding them in smoke that covered the "shrinking leaves and coarse rank flowers," and describing "mounds of ashes by the wayside."[106] He also describes them in *Hard Times*, which is set in the fictional manufacturing locale of Coketown.

It was a town of red brick, or of brick that would have been red if the smoke and ashes had allowed it. . . . It was a town of machinery and tall chimneys . . . [with] vast piles of buildings full of windows where . . . the piston of the steam-engine worked monotonously up and down like

The Black Country

Industrial towns such as Birmingham, Wolverhampton, and Manchester were the scenes of such severe air pollution in Victorian times that little could thrive. Dickens calls this region "The Black Country," and describes it in his novel *The Old Curiosity Shop.*

"They came by slow degrees upon a cheerless region, where not a blade of grass was seen to grow; where not a bud put forth its promise in the spring; where nothing green could live but on the surface of the stagnant pools, which here and there lay idly sweltering by the black roadside.

Advancing more and more into the shadow of this mournful place, its dark depressing influence . . . filled them with a dismal gloom. On every side, as far as the eye could see into the heavy distance, tall chimneys . . . poured out their plague of smoke, obscured the light, and made foul the melancholy air. . . . Dismantled houses here and there appeared, . . . unroofed, windowless, blackened, desolate, but yet inhabited. Men, women, children, wan in their looks and ragged in attire, tended the engines, fed their tributary fires, begged upon the road, or scowled half naked from the doorless houses, . . . and still, before, behind, and to the right and left was the same interminable perspective of brick towers, never ceasing in their black vomit, . . . shutting out the face of day, and closing in on all these horrors with a dense dark cloud."

Charles Dickens described the chimneys and smokestacks in manufacturing towns, such as Manchester (pictured), as "never ceasing in their black vomit."

the head of an elephant in a state of melancholy madness.[107]

The soot-filled air took a physical toll on everyone to a greater or lesser extent. Lung and skin diseases were common, particularly for those who worked in coal mines and textile mills. Even more prevalent, however, were the depression, alcoholism, and abuse that sprang directly from the constantly gray sky, the grimy surroundings, and the knowledge that escape from such conditions was impossible. In 1862, one visitor to England wrote, "A thick yellow fog fills the air, sinks, crawls on the very ground; . . . after an hour's walking one . . . can understand suicide."[108]

Louis Pasteur proved that microbes caused disease, a discovery that led to improved sanitation and disease prevention.

Combating Disease

When it came to combating the various diseases and ailments that plagued them, early Victorians were far from enlightened. Few understood the value of cleanliness in combating illness. Penicillin and antibiotics were unknown, and other disease-fighting weapons were primitive. Medicine was often a mixture of herbs and alcohol; those who could not afford that dosed patients with castor oil or warm gruel, then waited until they recovered or died. Public health services, which were becoming more common in London about 1840, offered some help; these often consisted of doctors who visited patients at home and instructed families to clean up the worst filth in their houses and neighborhoods.

Progress in the medical field was being made, however. Ether and chloroform made surgeries less harrowing; carbolic acid, though not widely used, lessened the risk of infection; and laudanum or opium eased the worst pain. In the 1850s, Dr. John Snow proved that cholera was carried in polluted drinking water, and later in the century, researcher Louis Pasteur proved that bacteria caused disease. A newly developed vaccine for smallpox became mandatory in 1853.

As time passed, greater numbers of hospitals and infirmaries were established in urban areas. Some facilities even provided isolation wards for those with contagious illnesses, but most patients entered them only as a last resort since conditions were filthy, service was primitive, and more patients died than survived their stay.

Last Resorts

Even if one was not sick, the sights and smells encountered upon entering a hospital were

The Hospital Patient

Hospitals were last resorts for the injured, sick, and dying in Dickens's day, and time spent within their walls was an upsetting experience even for the healthy. The author's visit to the casualty ward of a London hospital in the 1830s is recounted in *Sketches by Boz*.

"The dim light which burnt in the spacious room, increased rather than diminished the ghastly appearance of the hapless creatures in the beds, which were ranged in two long rows on either side. In one bed lay a child enveloped in bandages, with its body half consumed by fire; in another, a female, ren-dered hideous by some dreadful accident, was wildly beating her clenched fists on the coverlet, in pain; on a third, there lay stretched a young girl, apparently in the heavy stupor often the immediate precur-sor of death: her face was stained with blood, and her breast and arms were bound up in folds of linen. Two or three of the beds were empty, and their recent occu-pants were sitting beside them, but with faces so wan, and eyes so bright and glassy, that it was fearful to meet their gaze. On every face was stamped the expression of anguish and suffering."

nauseating, a combination of unbathed bodies, gangrenous wounds, and floors soaked with blood, urine, vomit, and other waste. Beds were uncomfortable and unsanitary. According to nursing pioneer Florence Nightingale, "It was common practice to put a new patient into the same sheets used by the last occupant of the bed, and mattresses were generally of flock, sodden and seldom if ever cleaned."[109] Prior to reforms started by Nightingale, nurses regularly allowed patients to become drunk to ease their pain, and wards were sometimes the scene of drunken arguments and brawls.

Medical treatments were rough and unsophisticated, carryovers from the days when anesthetics were unknown, and doctors had to be quick and strong enough to hold a patient down when performing an operation. Antiseptics were rarely used in the operating room, and doctors did not wash their hands or their instruments before surgery. Thus, infections were the rule, and many patients died of complications.

Doctors were often particularly lax in their treatment of the poor, since health problems were thought to be caused by laziness, dissipation, and coarse living. Prostitutes, who regularly suffered from malnutrition, consumption, and sexually transmitted diseases, received even poorer care. William Booth, founder of the Salvation Army, wrote:

[Their] life induced insanity, rheumatism, consumption, and all forms of syphilis. . . . In hospitals it is a known fact that these girls are not treated at all like other cases; they inspire disgust, and are most frequently discharged before being really cured.[110]

Death caused by accidents, starvation, disease, and natural events such as pregnancy and childbirth was common in Dickens's time, and death rates were considerably higher than they are today. In the 1830s, England's death rate was slightly over twenty-two deaths per thousand, with London's being at twenty-five per thousand or higher. Today's mortality rate in the United States is about nine per thousand. In some of the poorest districts, one-third of all babies died before their first birthday. Ironically, death rates were often highest in hospitals, where unsanitary practices spread infection from patient to patient.

Since accidents and illness were common occurrences, even the poorest Victorians planned ahead for their deaths. As it is today, dying was costly, and many sacrificed to pay for a dignified burial. Gillian Avery explains, "The Victorian poor saved not so much as an insurance against illness, but to cover the cost of their burial, to ensure that they were not buried by the parish as a pauper, a last hideous disgrace that it was worth starvation during one's life to avoid." [111]

"Pestiferous and Obscene"

Cemeteries were notorious sources of pollution in Dickens's time, since earlier generations had been ignorant of the danger stemming from careless burial practices. In London, many cemeteries were overcrowded and sat in the middle of residential neighborhoods. Dickens's mysterious character Nemo

Gravediggers prepare to bury a body. In London, cemeteries were so crowded that coffins were stacked on top of each other and bodies were placed in the ground next to remains from earlier burials.

in *Bleak House* is buried in such a locale, "a hemmed-in churchyard, pestiferous and obscene, whence malignant diseases are communicated to the bodies of our dear brothers and sisters who have not departed."[112] Nemo's case was common in inner-city London. Sanitary reformer Sir Edwin Chadwick stated in an 1830s report, "Closely surrounded by the abodes of the living, 20,000 adults and nearly 30,000 youths and children are every year imperfectly interred."[113]

Graveyards were not only poorly located but poorly drained, and wooden coffins could not contain decay. In some cemeteries, coffins were shallowly buried, even stacked on top of one another. Jo, the crossing sweep in *Bleak House*, describes one such burial. "They put him wery nigh the top. They was obliged to stamp upon it to git it in."[114] Reality was just as gruesome as Dickens's novels. The most callous grave diggers sometimes tossed bones from previous burials to one side to make room for new bodies, and in London, a horrified woman came upon four green, decomposing heads sticking out of the ground in one churchyard.

Interest in Reform

Dickens was one of the few Victorian novelists to write about the effects of pollution and disease in his day, but he was not alone in recognizing the growing threat to the public's health. Other reformers, some of them government officials like Edwin Chadwick, were also focusing on all kinds of social ills. Their initial efforts to correct such problems were often ineffective, and Dickens cynically suspected that their interest in reform would also be brief. In late 1854, during the Crimean War, he observed,

> It is more than ever necessary to keep their need of social Reforms before them at this time, for I clearly see that the war will be made an administration excuse for all sorts of shortcomings, and that nothing will have been done when the cholera comes again.[115]

Despite Dickens's pessimism, the country continued to change and improve as the century progressed. Significant reform was on the way, and in the end, it would make an enormous difference in everyone's lives.

Awakened Consciences

By the time Dickens was thirty, England's leaders and its people were growing increasingly aware of social ills that needed correction. Pollution was increasing. Poverty, crime, and disease were facts of life. Churches, private charities, and antivice societies were doing what they could to combat some of these problems, but they were fighting a losing battle.

There were people who argued that reforms were not the answer to all of the country's ills. Many Victorians felt that helping the needy sabotaged the economy, which theoretically rewarded hard work and punished sloth. Prior to becoming a reformer, Samuel Barnett remarked, "Indiscriminate charity [is] among the curses of London. . . . I would say that the poor starve because of the alms they receive. . . . The people never learn to work or save."[116] Others contended that there was something inherently, even genetically, wrong with the lower class that predisposed them to poverty. They felt that "bad characters created bad environments,"[117] and that the best anyone could do was lock up the lawbreakers and urge the rest to improve their lives.

Reformers such as Dickens disagreed with supporters of the status quo. He made the point that the poor needed education, improved sanitation, and better jobs rather than punishment. In 1870 Arnold Toynbee, who founded the Whitechapel Library and the Whitechapel Art Gallery in one of London's poor neighborhoods, publicly apologized to the poor for the injustices they had endured

for decades. "Instead of justice we have offered you charity, and instead of sympathy, we have offered you hard and unreal advice; but I think we are changing."[118]

Dickens and Charity

Even before Toynbee's time, England was changing. In 1800 just over 100 charitable organizations existed around the country; by the 1860s, there were almost 650, including those that provided practicalities such as shoes, food, and coal and those that set up orphanages, hospitals, and dispensaries.

Humanitarians such as Toynbee, Florence Nightingale, and William Booth of the Salvation Army actively promoted those causes they considered worthy. Dickens, a practical Christian who expressed his faith through his works, regularly gave money to needy friends and family, and he donated money, food, and clothes to strangers who wrote asking for aid. (He wisely checked first to ensure that they were truly in need.) He was particularly interested in helping abused women and children, as well as poverty-stricken artists, writers, and actors.

In 1843 Dickens formed a loose partnership with an old friend, millionairess Angela Burdett-Coutts, who needed an adviser to direct her choice of philanthropic projects. At Dickens's recommendation and with his help, Burdett-Coutts lent her support to several ragged schools and established Urania Cot-

Dickens was generous with his money, contributing to many worthy causes, but he sometimes grew tired of the never-ending demands made on his purse, as this letter to a friend, journalist William Henry Wills, illustrates. The passage is part of *Selected Letters of Charles Dickens*, edited by David Paroissien.

"Monday, Eleventh March, 1861
My Dear Wills,
I have had a begging letter from that Robert Barrow—a very bad one by the way—with an awful affectation of Christian piety in it . . . and the usual blaring assumption (of which I shall die at last) that I am immensely rich.
If you would not object to see him, I shall be very much obliged to you. . . . He seems to have no idea of my having already relieved him. I wish you would tell him that you have already given him 2 pounds and that you have 3 pounds more in hand; but that you must impress upon him in the strongest manner that he has no hope in making any further appeal to me . . . that I am quite weighed down and loaded and chained in life, by the enormous drags upon me . . . and that he must not deceive himself with the notion of my assisting him further. . . .
I declare to you that what with my mother—and [my brother] Alfred's family—and my wife—and a Saunders or so—I seem to stop sometimes like a steamer in a storm, and deliberate whether I shall go on whirling, or go down.—Ever faithfully."

tage, a residence for homeless women and reformed prostitutes in London. Dickens also provided support to Caroline Chisholm's Family Colonization Loan Society, an organization designed to help the poor emigrate to Australia and make a new start in life.

Government Reforms

Since Victorians traditionally depended on private efforts rather than legislation to improve society, parliamentary reforms were limited in the first half of the century. The 1832 Reform Act gave more men the vote and allowed the rapidly expanding middle class greater voice in government. The 1833 Factory Act limited working hours for children and created a system of factory inspections. The Coal Mines Act of 1842, sponsored by Lord Shaftesbury, prohibited women and children from being sent underground in the mines. Shaftesbury, a member of Parliament and a pioneer for reform, worked almost alone early in his career to improve the lot of the poor. He was an eloquent spokesperson for those who had no voice in government, and he drew national attention to many injustices that existed at the time.

As the century progressed and pollution and poverty increased, Parliament and other government agencies followed Shaftesbury's lead and became more aggressive in their reforms. Sir Edwin Chadwick, author of the Poor Law of 1834 and a member of the Poor Law Commission, which had been formed to organize and coordinate relief for the poor, spoke out for further reform in the 1840s. Ironically, Chadwick was one of the most hated men in England, since his legislation had established the despised workhouse system. He was concerned, however, that his

A government inspector investigates child labor in a factory in the 1880s. Child labor reforms began in the first half of the century, and they included limiting the hours a child could work and prohibiting children from working in coal mines.

initial plan had not decreased poverty, and so he continued to look for other solutions to the problem.

"Paved, Flagged, and Drained"

To Chadwick, disease and poor sanitary conditions were obvious factors that went hand in hand with poverty and kept the poor from finding work. Thus he set about investigating sanitation and disease by appointing several doctors to go out and survey conditions in neighborhoods with the highest death rates. They returned shocked and horrified by the squalor they had witnessed and by the danger they encountered there. One physician, Thomas Southwood Smith, observed, "During the last year . . . both relieving officers and medical men lost their lives in consequence of the brief stay in these places which they were obliged to make in the performances of their duties." [119]

From his own observations and those of Southwood Smith and others, Chadwick published a massive report in 1842, *Sanitary Condition of the Labouring Population of Great Britain*, which documented the overcrowding, filth, inadequate water supplies, and other grim conditions the Victorian poor endured. Chadwick suggested the formation of a national public-health authority to help provide clean water, improve drainage, and clean up neighborhoods.

Some denounced his plan, fearing its proposed changes were too radical and that it would take power away from local authorities. The threat of another cholera epidemic motivated Parliament to listen, however. In 1848, it passed the first British Public Health Act, which legislated the creation of a national general board of health, placed responsibility for drainage, water supplies, and inspections on town councils across the country, and gave them authority to raise taxes to pay for needed improvements.

Progress was slow but steady as industrial towns around the country began making changes. By 1861 Sir James Kay-Shuttleworth, secretary to the Manchester Board of Health, reported that in Manchester, "sewering had been undertaken, streets paved, flagged, and drained, the 352 streets named as being foul with refuse and stagnant pools had now almost disappeared, pigs had been driven out of houses, smoke from factories reduced, a proper water supply introduced." [120] Manchester reformers also created parks, founded a public library, and built public baths.

"Better Management of the Metropolis"

London, site of the worst sanitary problems in the country, was exempt from the nation's

Public Health Act since it was controlled by its municipal government. Recognizing the necessity of action, however, the mayor and his corporation passed a Sewers Act in 1848 that mandated improvements in waste disposal and a Metropolitan Water Act in 1852 that made water filtration compulsory. Londoners still drank water from the Thames River, but now that water was less polluted.

More changes came about in 1855 when the Metropolitan Board of Works was founded for "the better management of the metropolis in respect of the sewerage and drainage and the paving, cleansing, lighting and improvements thereof."[121] The board was unpopular with vestrymen and other local officials, but it did succeed in initiating change. After "the great stink" in 1858, the board's chief engineer Sir Joseph Bazalgette supervised the construction of over eighty miles of new sewers under the streets of London, effectively eliminating all open ditches, and connected them to newly designed underground drainage systems that carried waste outside London to outfall works. From there, it was released into the river at ebb tide and swept out to sea.

Bazalgette also engineered what became known as the Embankment, a series of massive walls made of granite, brick, and concrete, which edged part of the Thames that ran through London and allowed its polluted, muddy banks to be transformed into parks, gardens, and walking paths. At about the same time, the Board of Works took control of London's parks, including Hampstead Heath, Clapham Common, and Finsbury Park, and began road improvements that improved transportation and cleared away some of London's worst slum housing.

Sacred Rights of Property

Efforts by the Board of Works and other agencies to improve housing for the poor were less

"A Great and Good Man"

Anthony Ashley Cooper, the seventh earl of Shaftesbury, was one of few powerful noblemen who worked to improve the lot of the poor in Dickens's time. G. F. A. Best gives an overview of the Seventh Earl's contributions in his biography, *Shaftesbury*.

"Lord Shaftesbury spent a large part of his life rescuing poor people from two sets of circumstances over which they had little or no control: bad employers and bad living conditions. For many poor people, of course, these circumstances coincided. Their employers were bad, and the conditions they lived in were bad. If they had no employers at all . . . their living conditions might be so bad as to merit description as dying conditions. Shaftesbury knew all this. No other nobleman knew nearly as much about it. Few other men can have known much more. Shaftesbury became, during the eighteen-forties, one of the nation's experts on destitution. In Parliament he was looked to for authoritative speeches on it, and what he had to say was in the main exceedingly well worth listening to. . . . His activities in . . . education, welfare, housing, health, missions, mere human rescue and salvage work were of the highest value and importance, and . . . [marked] Shaftesbury as a great and good man."

successful than the board's sanitary reforms. Nevertheless, some advances were made. The Society for Improving the Condition of the Labouring Classes, founded by Lord Shaftesbury in the 1840s, and the Lodging House Act (Shaftesbury Act) of 1851 encouraged the construction of decent housing for poor working families; so did the Metropolitan Association for Improving the Dwellings of the Industrious Classes, founded in 1841. While these promoted construction of new dwellings, the poorest families could not afford even the cheapest, and so failed to benefit.

In 1868 the Artisans' Dwelling Act (Torrens Act) legislated the demolition of slums and the erection of new dwellings in London, but few funds were allocated for these projects. The Artisans' and Labourers' Dwelling Improvement Act (Cross Act) of 1875 made the city responsible for compensating land-lords if they wanted to improve their property. As a result, however, buildings were demolished, poor families displaced, and dishonest owners pocketed funds for rebuilding. In other cases, owners purposely allowed their property to deteriorate in order to get compensation. Statesman Joseph Chamberlain remarked in 1885, "The Torrens and Cross Acts are tainted and paralyzed by the incurable timidity with which Parliament is accustomed to deal with the sacred rights of property." [122]

Reform Efforts for Housing and Children

Too impatient to wait for more effective reforms, Dickens and Angela Burdett-Coutts began their own limited program of housing renewal in 1856. As biographer Hesketh Pearson writes:

A view of the London Bridge and the busy Thames River. The Sewers Act and the Metropolitan Water Act decreased pollution and made the Thames a safer water source for Londoners.

Though a few reforms provided apartments for the laboring class in London (top), Charles Dickens (bottom) and Angela Burdett-Coutts believed them to be insufficient and began their own housing project.

They went down to Bethnal Green, and picked on a spot known as Nova Scotia Gardens, which was nothing but a vast dung heap, played upon by the dirty, ragged, barefooted children of thieves and prostitutes. The place was cleaned up, and by 1862 Columbia Square, four blocks of model flats, had been built. . . . All this was pioneer work, and Dickens spent as much time on it as if he had nothing else to do.[123]

Flats, or apartments, were seen by some to be the future of lower-class housing. They were space saving—one to three rooms per flat, four flats per floor—and relatively inexpensive to build. The best had running water and a water-closet, although often these facilities were communal and located at the end of a corridor on each floor. Dickens and Burdett-Coutts ensured that Columbia Square apartments would be well ventilated by creating corridor windows that were permanently open, spacious halls, and doors located to encourage air flow. They also kept their rent low, so that "the very poorest of the industrious classes,"[124] could afford decent housing.

Flats were an improvement over the ramshackle rookeries, but overall they were not the perfect solution to England's housing problems. Burdett-Coutts's were attractive as well as affordable, but others were expensive, cramped, and gloomy. Residents who scraped up the money to live in them soon discovered that they had been victimized again, since cheaply built structures quickly deteriorated and were not maintained by careless landlords.

While many reformers focused on sanitation, health, and housing in the mid-1800s, others made children their focus. In addition

Previously a privilege for upper-class children, education became more available with the establishment of the Ragged School Union in 1844 and a legal right when elementary education became mandatory in 1870.

to laws that limited children's work hours and outlawed females in coal mines, legislation passed in 1840 and 1864 was designed to end the exploitation of young boys apprenticed to be chimney sweeps. Master sweeps and property owners ignored the law, however, and the practice continued until five years after Dickens's death.

As a result of Lord Shaftesbury's efforts, the Ragged School Union was formed in 1844 and increasing numbers of poor children attended school. In 1870, the year of Dickens's death, Parliament passed the Education Act, which made elementary education mandatory for all children. New schools were built and

locally elected school boards were put in charge of enforcing the new law. Historian Ivor Brown observes, "The start was slow, the progress was slow, but a disgrace to the nation had been partially ended."[125]

Great Benefactor

Thomas J. Barnardo, a champion of destitute children in the Victorian era, was also interested in education, but his commitment to youth extended to other aspects of their welfare as well. Barnardo, a London physician, began his career in Stepney, one of London's poor neighborhoods, where he witnessed first-hand the problems poor children faced. Convinced that most had the potential to become responsible citizens, he devoted his career to them and others across the city, finding foster homes for some, establishing day schools that served hot breakfasts and dinners four days a week, caring for the sick, injured, and physically handicapped, even helping young criminals make fresh starts in Canada or Australia.

On daily walks around London, Barnardo regularly took "waifs and strays" off the streets, and rescued "poor bairns from impending ruin."[126] He also handed out clothes and money for food and medical care. Learning that the poor often pawned new clothes and used the money to buy alcohol, he instituted a loan system in which boots and other items were stamped with an indelible mark. Barnardo's mark became well-known in poor neighborhoods, and anyone trying to sell such items risked being charged with theft.

Barnardo was not enormously wealthy, and he was unable to support a vast number of projects on his own income. He had many contacts with the well-to-do, however, and never hesitated to ask them to give generously to his causes. One of Barnardo's biographers writes:

> Many of the ease-loving affluent Victorians came to loathe him. His policy of direct personal approach in their own homes brought 'the smell of the slums into the drawing-rooms'. He touched their consciences and their pockets, and they resented it. Fortunately many more were fired by his compassion and gave willingly to the cause.[127]

Progress and the Skeptic

By 1870, the year of Dickens's death, social improvements were well under way in England. Deaths from typhus, dysentery, and cholera decreased as drinking water became cleaner and drains more efficient. Paving projects eliminated the worst of the dust and mud in

Unwanted Philanthropy

Few of the poor wanted help from philanthropists who patronized, offered unwanted advice, but gave little practical assistance. In Dickens's *Bleak House*, a destitute brick maker speaks his mind to Mrs. Pardiggle, the neighborhood philanthropist who has intruded into his home and criticized his lifestyle.

"Now you're a-going to poll-pry and question according to custom. . . . I'll save you the trouble. Is my daughter a-washin? Yes, she *is* a-washin. Look at the water. Smell it! that's wot we drinks. How do you like it, and what do you think of gin, instead! An't

my place dirty? Yes, it is dirty—it's nat'rally dirty, and it's nat'rally onwholesome; and we've had five . . . onwholesome children, as is all dead infants, and so much the better for them, and for us besides. . . . How have I been conducting of myself? Why, I've been drunk for three days; and I'd a been drunk four, if I'd a had the money. Don't I never mean for to go to church? No, I don't never mean for to go to church. I shouldn't be expected there if I did; the beadle's too genteel for me. And how did my wife get that black eye? Why, I give it her; and if she says I didn't, she's a Lie."

*An 1875 illustration of the poor receiving food in a religious almshouse.
Charities such as this sprang up in the nineteenth century as England became
more aware of its disadvantaged citizens.*

the streets. In response to public protest, live-stock markets and related industries in London were moved to new locales outside the city. New legislation forbade further burials in over-crowded graveyards, and new cemeteries were constructed that were well drained, enclosed, landscaped, and properly managed.

To help the poor, religious and charitable organizations provided a variety of services from soup kitchens to seaside outings for chil-dren. William Booth established his Christian Mission in 1865, renaming it the Salvation Army in 1878. At the opposite end of the philosophical spectrum, German philosopher and revolutionary Karl Marx, a political exile living in London, founded the International Workingmen's Association in 1864, an organi-zation dedicated to improving the welfare of the working classes.

Dickens lived to see many of these re-forms, but even they did not satisfy him. Soci-ety had become more aware of its own shortcomings, but in his eyes, too little had been accomplished. Thus, while he lived, Dickens continued to do what he knew best—write. In his writing, he stressed a theme that became more emphatic as time passed: Poverty and social oppression were twin evils that should not be tolerated by civ-ilized men and women anywhere.

Dickens's Legacy

As Charles Dickens grew older and more impatient with England's established social order, he wrote openly and angrily of the materialism that characterized the industrial world. *Hard Times*, written in 1854, is his bitterest novel. In it he lashed out against political and economic policies that ignored generosity, tolerance, and compassion and claimed that the "pursuit of individual fortune benefits society as a whole."[128] To Dickens, such policies were merely justifications for selfishness.

> Into all relations . . . of this life, there must enter something of feeling and sentiment; something of mutual explanation, forbearance, and consideration; something . . . not exactly stateable in figures; otherwise those relations are wrong and rotten at the core and will never bear sound fruit.[129]

A Stern Warning

Dickens never hesitated to exaggerate society's shortcomings and play on people's emotions in order to gain sympathy and support for his views. Hesketh Pearson writes, "His nature was such that when he saw inhumanity, or injustice, or indifference, he did not bother his head with the whys and wherefores: he simply exposed and attacked it with burning zeal."[130] Despite this emotional approach, however, he disliked and distrusted movements such as Chartism, communism, socialism, and the like, which appealed to workers' feelings and sometimes relied

The Gradgrind Philosophy

Dickens was his angriest in *Hard Times*, in which he condemned utilitarianism—a popular belief in which all ideas, actions, and situations were judged solely by their usefulness. In the novel, Dickens expresses his cynicism through the character of Mr. Gradgrind, whose utilitarian philosophy eventually leads to tragedy.

"It was a fundamental principle of the Gradgrind philosophy that everything was to be paid for. Nobody was ever on any account to give anybody anything, or render anybody help without purchase. Gratitude was to be abolished, and the virtues springing from it were not to be. Every inch of the existence of mankind, from birth to death, was to be a bargain across the counter. And if we didn't get to Heaven that way, it was not a politico-economical place, and we had no business there."

Charles Dickens in the study of his Gad's Hill home. Dickens had always used his writing to expose society's ills, and his commentaries became increasingly bitter as he grew older.

heavily on peer pressure and violence to make their points.

Dickens rejected organized insurrection as a means of change, but riots and mob violence appear in some of his writings. In *The Old Curiosity Shop*, he writes of a time when "maddened men, armed with sword and firebrand . . . rushed forth on errands of terror and destruction."[131] In *Barnaby Rudge*, he creates a mob made up of desperate, miserable human beings, almost totally ignorant of the cause they are supporting. In *A Tale of Two Cities*, he paints the downtrodden masses of the French Revolution with a dark brush, letting them rage out of control until they are as callous and cruel as their former oppressors. The inclusion of such scenes in his novels served as his warning to those in power: Your indifference will be your ruin if those you oppress turn to violence to right their wrongs.

The Storyteller

As he focused on topics ranging from America to alcoholism, wages to workhouses, Dick-

ens's pen was his sword, and he wielded it tirelessly throughout his lifetime. Hesketh Pearson describes,

> In his own sphere he attended to everything, showing why peace societies were foolish and why disarmament was reckless, attacking all forms of oppression, deriding every sort of cant [insincerity], ridiculing stupidity, exposing cruelty, hitting at this, laughing at that.[132]

Dickens also spent months on book tours, during which he read portions of his novels aloud to large audiences. Between April 1858 and March 1870 he gave over four hundred readings, with the proceeds of many of them going to charity. Listeners soon realized that Dickens's talent for storytelling was as extraordinary as his ability to write. Alone on the stage he brought such life to a scene that his audience sat spellbound. His friend, essayist and historian Thomas Carlyle remarked, "I had no conception, before hearing Dickens read, of what capacities lie in the human face and voice. No theatre-stage could have had more players than seemed to flit about his face, and all tones were present. There was no need of any orchestra."[133]

Career's End

Due to age and an exhausting schedule, by 1866 Charles Dickens's remarkable physical energy was waning. Despite that, he remained editor of his weekly magazine *All the Year Round*, the successor to *Household Words*, and worked steadily on a final novel, *The Mystery of Edwin Drood*, which he never completed. He ignored his doctor's advice and went on a lengthy tour of America in 1867, giving dozens of readings, then returned to England for a final reading tour in late 1868 and early 1869.

On June 8, 1870, while at Gad's Hill Place, his country home, he suffered a stroke from which he never recovered consciousness. Dickens died the next day at the age of fifty-eight, leaving a world of readers to mourn his passing.

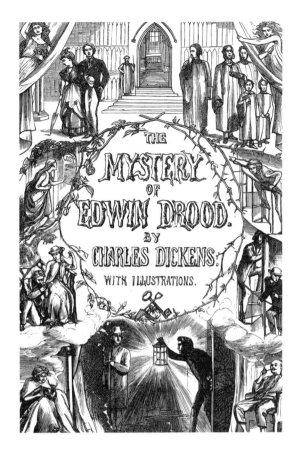

Dickens's last projects were writing The Mystery of Edwin Drood *(the novel's title page is shown above) and going on tour reading his books to audiences (left).*

He was buried with highest honors in Westminster Abbey, final resting place of heroes and kings. Novelist John Irving observed, "There were . . . thousands of mourners who came to pay their respects to the former child-laborer whose toil had once seemed so menial in the blacking warehouse at Hungerford Stairs."[134]

"One of the Greatest Writers of the World"

The popularity of Dickens's novels has endured from the early days of his career to the present, but few literary scholars recognized or appreciated the depth of his talent until decades after his death. Critics acknowledged his skill in plotting and even admitted that he was a sharp-eyed observer of the Victorian scene, but they persisted in seeing his work as simple entertainment, complaining that he relied too much on sentiment, humor, and coincidence. Even his friend Thomas Carlyle went so far as to say, "Dickens has not written anything which will be found of much use in solving the problems of life. But he is worth something; worth a penny to read of an evening before going to bed."[135]

As time passed, however, scholars and critics came to recognize the author as a major talent in the literary world, a man whose depth and complexity was reflected in his work. Nobel Prize–winner George Bernard Shaw wrote after the turn of the century, "He is, by the pure force of genius one of the greatest writers of the world. . . . There is no 'greatest book' of Dickens; all his books form one great life-work . . . all are magnificent."[136] And biographer Edgar Johnson writes, "He was one of the heroes of art, not merely battling the unpastured dragons of life's waste, but enriching and creating a world."[137]

Killing Nancy

Dickens's book tours took an enormous toll on his energies, but he persisted in giving them. His determination to enact the murder scene from *Oliver Twist*, with all its suspense and violence, possibly contributed to his early death, but it was a never-to-be-forgotten experience for his audience, as Hesketh Pearson describes in *Dickens, His Character, Comedy, and Career.*

"The reading began with the scene where Fagin tells Noah Claypole to watch Nancy. Then came the meeting on London Bridge where Nancy gives Fagin away; by which time, such was the skill of Dickens, all the characters were alive in the listener's imagination. After that Noah recounts what he has heard to Sikes; the killing of Nancy followed, and the performance ended with the flight of the criminal. From a quiet beginning, Dickens imparted to the murder scene such a sense of horror that the audience were semi-paralysed, and sat with blanched faces in frozen silence. The shrieks of Nancy rang through the hall in a frightening falsetto, and at the conclusion of the episode no one stirred, no one seemed to breathe. The haunted murderer's 'thick-coming fancies' were a fitting finale, and the reading closed on a note of doom. It was a searching experience; no one who heard it ever forgot it, and none but the hardiest went a second time."

Visitors gaze upon Charles Dickens's grave in Westminster Abbey. During Dickens's lifetime, many reforms were set in motion to improve life for the oppressed in England's society.

The Dignity of Man

Many "dragons" that Dickens battled more than a century ago—poverty, ignorance, indifference—still plague society today. Some of his deepest convictions, that the poor have a right to decent homes and jobs, that the government should be more responsive to the voice of the working class, that education is a passport to a better life, are echoed by contemporary thinkers. In that sense, his work is timeless, a lively reminder to generations of readers that societal ills are perpetual, and that solutions can be found when people of all backgrounds recognize their mutual problems and work together for the common good.

More than a century has passed since Charles Dickens's death. In the words of his biographer, Edgar Johnson:

His passionate heart has long crumbled to dust. But the world he created shines with undying life, and the hearts of men still vibrate to his indignant anger, his love, his tears, his glorious laughter, and his triumphant faith in the dignity of man.[138]

Notes

Introduction: "A Terrible Boy to Read"

1. Quoted in Hesketh Pearson, *Dickens, His Character, Comedy, and Career*. New York: Harper & Bros., 1949, p. 7.
2. Quoted in J. B. Priestley, *Charles Dickens: A Pictorial Biography*. New York: Viking Press, 1962, p. 12.
3. Quoted in Pearson, *Dickens, His Character, Comedy, and Career*, p. 3.
4. Quoted in Pearson, *Dickens, His Character, Comedy, and Career*, p. 4.
5. Quoted in Pearson, *Dickens, His Character, Comedy, and Career*, pp. 17–18.
6. Quoted in Pearson, *Dickens, His Character, Comedy, and Career*, p. 67.

Chapter 1: England and the Early Victorians

7. Henry Mayhew, *London Labour and the London Poor*, vol. 3. London: Griffin, Bohn, 1861, pp. 302–303.
8. Quoted in Roy Porter, *London: A Social History*. Cambridge, MA: Harvard University Press, 1995, p. 197.
9. Charles Dickens, *Dombey and Son*. Oxford: Oxford University Press, 1987, p. 281.
10. Charles Dickens, *Sketches by Boz*, ed. Michael Slater. Columbus: Ohio State University Press, 1994, p. 505.
11. Charles Dickens, *Bleak House*. New York: Bantam Books, 1983, p. 523.
12. Quoted in Pearson, *Dickens, His Character, Comedy, and Career*, p. 328.
13. Quoted in Porter, *London: A Social History*, p. 240.
14. Porter, *London: A Social History*, p. 257.

15. Quoted in Edgar Johnson, *Charles Dickens*, vol. 1. New York: Simon & Schuster, 1952, p. 452.
16. Quoted in Gillian Avery, *Victorian People*. New York: Holt, Rinehard & Winston, 1970, p. 13.
17. Quoted in Johnson, *Charles Dickens*, vol. 1, p. 534.

Chapter 2: City Men and Climbing Boys

18. Charles Dickens, *Little Dorrit*. Oxford: Oxford University Press, 1988, p. 90.
19. Charles Dickens, *Hard Times*. Oxford: Oxford University Press, 1989, p. 18.
20. Dickens, *Hard Times*, p. 182.
21. Quoted in Porter, *London: A Social History*, p. 275.
22. Quoted in William J. Fishman, *East End 1888*. Philadelphia: Temple University Press, 1988, p. 73.
23. Quoted in Millicent Rose, *The East End of London*. London: Cresset Press, 1951, p. 187.
24. Mayhew, *London Labour and the London Poor*, vol. 3, p. 304.
25. Quoted in Rose, *The East End of London*, p. 197.
26. Quoted in Porter, *London: A Social History*, p. 284.
27. Quoted in John Thomson, *Victorian London Street Life*. New York: Dover Publications, 1994, p. 91.
28. Rose, *The East End of London*, p. 193.
29. Charles Dickens, *Our Mutual Friend*. New York: New American Library, 1964, p. 28.
30. Quoted in Porter, *London: A Social History*, p. 286.

31. Mayhew, *London Labour and the London Poor*, vol. 2, p. 154.
32. Charles Dickens, *Oliver Twist*. Oxford: Oxford University Press, 1985, p. 26.
33. Quoted in Ivor Brown, *Dickens in His Time*. London: Thomas Nelson and Sons, 1963, p. 52.
34. Dickens, *Bleak House*, p. 204.

Chapter 3: Londoners at Their Firesides

35. Quoted in Porter, *London: A Social History*, pp. 257–58.
36. Dickens, *Bleak House*, p. 203.
37. Quoted in Porter, *London: A Social History*, p. 213.
38. Dickens, *Sketches by Boz*, p. 94.
39. Charles Dickens, *Martin Chuzzlewit*. London: Mandarin Paperbacks, 1991, p. 163.
40. Dickens, *Sketches by Boz*, p. 279.
41. Dickens, *Sketches by Boz*, p. 316.
42. Dickens, *Martin Chuzzlewit*, p. 139.
43. Avery, *Victorian People*, p. 129.
44. Dickens, *Little Dorrit*, p. 24.
45. Dickens, *Sketches by Boz*, pp. 281–82.
46. Avery, *Victorian People*, p. 189–90.
47. Quoted in Porter, *London: A Social History*, p. 232.
48. Charles Dickens, *A Tale of Two Cities*. New York: Scholastic, 1962, p. 63.
49. Dickens, *Sketches by Boz*, pp. 262, 264.
50. Dickens, *Sketches by Boz*, pp. 72–73.
51. Dickens, *Bleak House*, p. 204.
52. Dickens, *Sketches by Boz*, pp. 74–75.
53. Quoted in Fishman, *East End 1888*, p. 34.
54. Quoted in Avery, *Victorian People*, p. 218.
55. Quoted in Fishman, *East End 1888*, p. 126.
56. Dickens, *Our Mutual Friend*, p. 227.
57. Dickens, *Hard Times*, p. 30.
58. Dickens, *Little Dorrit*, p. 23.
59. Quoted in Porter, *London: A Social History*, p. 297.

Chapter 4: Too Knocked About to Learn

60. Quoted in Johnson, *Charles Dickens*, vol. 2, p. 1,100.
61. Quoted in Brown, *Dickens in His Time*, p. 157.
62. Quoted in Avery, *Victorian People*, p. 118.
63. Quoted in Brown, *Dickens in His Time*, p. 158.
64. Charles Dickens, *Nicholas Nickleby*. Oxford: Oxford University Press, 1990, pp. 30, 77.
65. Charles Dickens, *David Copperfield*. Oxford: Oxford University Press, 1981, pp. 71, 75.
66. Quoted in Johnson, *Charles Dickens*, vol. 2, p. 635.
67. Dickens, *Nicholas Nickleby*, p. 97.
68. Dickens, *David Copperfield*, p. 194.
69. Quoted in Brown, *Dickens in His Time*, p. 165.
70. Quoted in Avery, *Victorian People*, p. 122.
71. Dickens, *Little Dorrit*, p. 377.
72. Charles Dickens, *The Old Curiosity Shop*. New York: Dodd, Mead, 1946, p. 234.
73. Quoted in Avery, *Victorian People*, p. 101.
74. Quoted in Porter, *London: A Social History*, p. 297.
75. Charles Dickens, *Great Expectations*. New York: Bantam Books, 1986, pp. 39–40.
76. Quoted in Porter, *London: A Social History*, p. 297.
77. Dickens, *Great Expectations*, p. 42.
78. Quoted in Avery, *Victorian People*, pp. 230–31.

Chapter 5: Palaces of Retribution

79. Porter, *London: A Social History*, p. 299.
80. Dickens, *Oliver Twist*, p. 297.
81. Rose, *The East End of London*, p. 214.
82. Quoted in Rose, *The East End of London*, pp. 53–54.
83. Dickens, *Oliver Twist*, pp. 137–38.
84. Quoted in Avery, *Victorian People*, p. 230.
85. Dickens, *Oliver Twist*, p. 115.
86. Quoted in Porter, *London: A Social History*, p. 249.
87. Dickens, *Sketches by Boz*, p. 207.
88. Quoted in Avery, *Victorian People*, p. 232.
89. Charles Dickens, *The Pickwick Papers*. Oxford: Oxford University Press, 1987, p. 595.
90. Quoted in Michael Ignatieff, *A Just Measure of Pain*. New York: Pantheon, 1978, p. 34.
91. Brown, *Dickens in His Time*, p. 61.
92. Dickens, *Sketches by Boz*, p. 199.
93. Quoted in Ignatieff, *A Just Measure of Pain*, p. 177.
94. Dickens, *Great Expectations*, pp. 152–53.
95. Quoted in Ignatieff, *A Just Measure of Pain*, p. 91.
96. Dickens, *Great Expectations*, p. 36.
97. Quoted in Brown, *Dickens in His Time*, p. 213.

Chapter 6: Dustheaps and Disease

98. Quoted in Porter, *London: A Social History*, p. 259.
99. Dickens, *Bleak House*, p. 1.
100. Dickens, *Hard Times*, p. 28.
101. Quoted in Porter, *London: A Social History*, p. 260.
102. Quoted in Porter, *London: A Social History*, p. 265.
103. Dickens, *Bleak House*, p. 1.
104. Dickens, *Great Expectations*, p. 14.
105. Quoted in Avery, *Victorian People*, p. 195.
106. Dickens, *The Old Curiosity Shop*, pp. 336–37.
107. Dickens, *Hard Times*, p. 28.
108. Quoted in Porter, *London: A Social History*, p. 279.
109. Quoted in Guy Williams, *The Age of Miracles*. Chicago: Academy Chicago Publishers, 1987, p. 90.
110. Quoted in Fishman, *East End 1888*, p. 124.
111. Avery, *Victorian People*, p. 199.
112. Dickens, *Bleak House*, p. 140.
113. Quoted in Porter, *London: A Social History*, p. 273.
114. Dickens, *Bleak House*, p. 209.
115. Charles Dickens, *Selected Letters of Charles Dickens*, ed. David Paroissien. Boston: Twayne Publishers, 1985, p. 263.

Chapter 7: Awakened Consciences

116. Quoted in Fishman, *East End 1888*, p. 230.
117. Porter, *London: A Social History*, p. 271.
118. Quoted in Porter, *London: A Social History*, p. 304.
119. Quoted in Porter, *London: A Social History*, p. 261.
120. Quoted in Avery, *Victorian People*, pp. 185–86.
121. Quoted in Porter, *London: A Social History*, p. 263.
122. Quoted in Porter, *London: A Social History*, p. 270.
123. Pearson, *Dickens, His Character, Comedy, and Career*, p. 201.
124. Quoted in Rose, *The East End of London*, p. 258.

125. Brown, *Dickens in His Time*, p. 150.
126. Quoted in Fishman, *East End 1888*, p. 236.
127. Quoted in Fishman, *East End 1888*, p. 245.

Chapter 8: Dickens's Legacy

128. Paul Schlicke, Introduction to Dickens, *Hard Times*, p. xiii.
129. Quoted in Schlicke, Introduction to *Hard Times*, p. xiv.
130. Pearson, *Dickens, His Character, Comedy, and Career*, p. 194.
131. Dickens, *The Old Curiosity Shop*, p. 337.
132. Pearson, *Dickens, His Character, Comedy, and Career*, p. 176.
133. Quoted in Pearson, *Dickens, His Character, Comedy, and Career*, p. 271.
134. John Irving, Introduction to Dickens, *Great Expectations*, p. xxviii.
135. Quoted in Pearson, *Dickens, His Character, Comedy, and Career*, p. 195.
136. Quoted in Johnson, *Charles Dickens*, vol. 2, p. 1,140.
137. Johnson, *Charles Dickens*, vol. 2, p. 1,141.
138. Johnson, *Charles Dickens*, vol. 2, p. 1,158.

For Further Reading

Ivor Brown, *Dickens in His Time*. London: Thomas Nelson and Sons, 1963. Well-written account of Dickens's England with chapters on politics, prisons, travel, schools, and reforms.

Charles Dickens, *David Copperfield*. Oxford: Oxford University Press, 1981. Dickens's most personal novel relates the coming of age of a young man in Victorian times.

——, *Oliver Twist*. Oxford: Oxford University Press, 1985. The tale of a young boy's adventures with a band of criminals in early Victorian London.

——, *Sketches by Boz*. Ed. Michael Slater. Columbus: Ohio State University Press, 1994. Dickens's first work includes short articles on a variety of topics such as next-door neighbors, gin shops, hospitals, and Parliament.

John Thomson, *Victorian London Street Life*. New York: Dover Publications, 1994. Originally published in 1877, this book contains historic photos and accompanying articles on such colorful Victorian occupations as Covent Garden flower women, London cabmen, flying dustmen, and others.

Works Consulted

Gillian Avery, *Victorian People*. New York: Holt, Rinehard & Winston, 1970. An overview of the Victorian age, with chapters devoted to the aristocracy, the middle class, cities and industry, poverty, and criminals; includes period illustrations from Victorian magazines and newspapers such as *Punch*, the *Illustrated London News*, and others.

G. F. A. Best, *Shaftesbury*. New York: Arco Publishing, 1964. The life and accomplishments of statesman and reformer Lord Ashley, the seventh earl of Shaftesbury.

Charles Dickens, *Bleak House*. New York: Bantam Books, 1983. Dickens weaves a story around the fictional legal case of *Jardyce vs. Jardyce* to make his point about the evils of England's slow-moving legal system.

———, *Dombey and Son*. Oxford: Oxford University Press, 1987. The story of a selfish egoist whose pride stops him from experiencing the warmth and joy of human love.

———, *Great Expectations*. New York: Bantam Books, 1986. Pip, a poor boy, is educated to be a gentleman at the bequest of a mysterious benefactor.

———, *Hard Times*. Oxford: Oxford University Press, 1989. Dickens exposes the evils of materialism and utilitarianism while he tells the tragic story of Louisa Gradgrind and her father.

———, *Little Dorrit*. Oxford: Oxford University Press, 1988. The author campaigns against materialism and snobbery as represented by the rich Merdle family and ridicules government inefficiency by creating the fictional "Circumlocution Office."

———, *Martin Chuzzlewit*. London: Mandarin Paperbacks, 1991. Written after Dickens's first visit to the United States, the novel drew the wrath of many American readers for its sharp critique of American manners.

———, *Nicholas Nickleby*. Oxford: Oxford University Press, 1990. Dickens's exposé of greedy proprietors of private boarding schools who brutalized their students and taught them little or nothing.

———, *The Old Curiosity Shop*. New York: Dodd, Mead, 1946. The author uses industrial conflict and England's Black Country as a horrifying backdrop for his story of the adventures of little Nell and her grandfather; Victorian readers enjoyed the tale, but modern readers find it too sentimental.

———, *Our Mutual Friend*. New York: New American Library, 1964. Dickens tells the story of the Golden Dustman and attacks the values of the newly rich.

———, *The Pickwick Papers*. Oxford: Oxford University Press, 1987. The novel that brought Dickens fame when he was only twenty-five tells of the humorous adventures and misadventures of a group of slightly eccentric individuals.

———, *Selected Letters of Charles Dickens*. Ed. David Paroissien. Boston: Twayne Publishers, 1985. A selection of Dickens's personal and business correspondence from 1832 through 1869; includes topics such as family, philanthropy, writing, and public life.

————, *A Tale of Two Cities*. New York: Scholastic, 1962. A tale of love and loyalty set in London and Paris during the French Revolution of 1789.

William J. Fishman, *East End 1888*. Philadelphia: Temple University Press, 1988. Focusing on Victorian England almost two decades after Dickens' death, the book nevertheless contains much information on conditions that existed in England throughout the entire nineteenth century.

Michael Ignatieff, *A Just Measure of Pain*. New York: Pantheon, 1978. An account of England's penal system in the eighteenth and nineteenth centuries.

Edgar Johnson, *Charles Dickens*. Volumes 1–2. New York: Simon & Schuster, 1952. The story of Charles Dickens, including critiques of his novels and details of his life not found in other works.

Henry Mayhew, *London Labour and the London Poor*. Volumes 1–3. London: Griffin, Bohn, 1861. An eyewitness account of the living and working conditions of the London poor and laboring class; Mayhew's work is considered the most complete and definitive of the time.

Francis Miltoun, *Dickens' London*. Boston: L. C. Page, 1903. An account of Dickens's life, his works, his contemporaries, and early Victorian London; difficult to read.

Hesketh Pearson, *Dickens, His Character, Comedy, and Career*. New York: Harper & Bros., 1949. Biography of Dickens with emphasis on personal experiences that colored his writing.

Roy Porter, *London: A Social History*. Cambridge, MA: Harvard University Press, 1995. A study of London from its beginning to modern times; contains valuable chapters on the growth of the city during the industrial revolution, details of Victorian life, and social and political problems and reforms during that time.

J. B. Priestley, *Charles Dickens: A Pictorial Biography*. New York: Viking Press, 1962. A short but readable biography of Dickens by a renowned British author and journalist.

Millicent Rose, *The East End of London*. London: Cresset Press, 1951. A history of the East End of London, notorious for its slums, poverty, and criminal element; includes information on jobs, pastimes, homes, and customs of those who lived there in the 1800s.

Guy Williams, *The Age of Miracles*. Chicago: Academy Chicago Publishers, 1987. Short but fascinating account of the history of medicine and medical treatment in the nineteenth century.

Angus Wilson, *The World of Dickens*. New York: Viking Press, 1970. A biography of the novelist, including quotes from his letters and writings, and short résumés of his novels.

Index

Picture Credits

About the Author

Diane Yancey is the author of many books for Lucent, including *Life in War-Torn Bosnia*, *Life in the Elizabethan Theater*, *Life in a Japanese American Internment Camp*, and *Union Generals of the Civil War*. She has also written *Desperadoes and Dynamite*, an account of train robbery in the United States; *The Hunt for Hidden Killers*, ten tales of medical detection; and *Camels for Uncle Sam*, the story of a daring army experiment that brought camels to the United States prior to the Civil War.

In addition to her interest in writing, the author enjoys collecting old books, traveling, and enjoying life in the Pacific Northwest with her husband, two daughters, and two cats.